CROSSWORDS

FOR KIDS

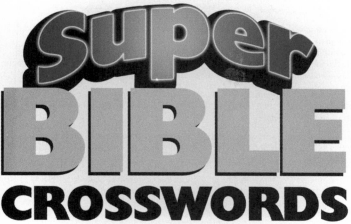

CROSSWORDS

BARBOUR
PUBLISHING

Our mission is to publish and distribute inspirational products offering exceptional value and biblical encouragement to the masses.

Member of the
Evangelical Christian
Publishers Association

Printed in the United States of America.

INTRODUCTION

Hey, kids—

Looking for something to do on a rainy afternoon, a long car ride, or a night when there's nothing to watch on TV? Then you've come to the right place!

Super Bible Crosswords for Kids is packed with more than 160 fun puzzles. As you solve them, you'll be learning important truth from the Bible—and what could be better than that?

There are two sections in *Super Bible Crosswords for Kids*. Part 1 starts on the next page and offers 83 puzzles based on the Bible's book of John. Part 2 is all about prayer, with another 81 puzzles. Answers for all the puzzles follow, beginning on page 339.

But enough of the talk. We know you're ready to begin, so jump on in. Enjoy!

THE WORD

FROM: JOHN 1:1–5, NASB

ACROSS

1. "IN THE ___God___ WAS THE WORD."
2. "AND THE ___word___ WAS WITH GOD."
3. "AND THE WORD WAS _God_."
4. "__he__ WAS IN THE BEGINNING WITH GOD."

DOWN

1. "ALL _things_ CAME INTO BEING THROUGH HIM."
2. "IN HIM WAS _life_."
3. "AND THE LIFE WAS THE _light_ OF MEN."
4. "AND THE _darkness_ DID NOT COMPREHEND IT."

CHILDREN OF GOD

JOHN 1:10–13, KJV

USING THE UNDERLINED WORDS BELOW, FILL IN THE BOXES ON THE NEXT PAGE.

"HE WAS IN THE <u>WORLD</u>, AND THE WORLD WAS <u>MADE</u> BY HIM, AND THE WORLD KNEW HIM NOT."

"<u>HE</u> <u>CAME</u> UNTO HIS OWN, AND HIS OWN <u>RECEIVED</u> HIM NOT. "

"BUT AS MANY AS RECEIVED HIM, TO THEM GAVE HE POWER TO BECOME THE <u>SONS</u> OF GOD, EVEN TO THEM THAT <u>BELIEVE</u> ON HIS NAME: WHICH WERE <u>BORN</u>, NOT OF <u>BLOOD</u>, <u>NOR</u> OF THE <u>WILL</u> OF THE FLESH, NOR OF THE WILL OF MAN, BUT OF GOD."

GRACE AND TRUTH

JOHN 1:14

ACROSS

1. "THE WORD BECAME _____."
2. "AND   MADE   HIS   _____."
3. "_____ US."
4. "WE HAVE SEEN HIS _____."

DOWN

1. "THE GLORY OF THE ONE AND ONLY, WHO
   CAME _____."
2. "THE _____."
3. "_____ OF."
4. "_____ AND TRUTH."

11

JESUS COMES TO EARTH

JOHN 1:16–18

USING THE UNDERLINED WORDS BELOW,
FILL IN THE BOXES ON THE NEXT PAGE.

"FROM <u>THE</u> FULLNESS OF HIS <u>GRACE</u> WE
HAVE ALL RECEIVED ONE <u>BLESSING</u> AFTER
ANOTHER."

"FOR THE LAW WAS <u>GIVEN</u> THROUGH <u>MOSES</u>;
GRACE AND <u>TRUTH</u> CAME THROUGH <u>JESUS</u>
CHRIST."

"NO ONE HAS EVER SEEN <u>GOD</u>, BUT GOD THE
ONE AND ONLY, WHO IS AT THE FATHER'S
<u>SIDE</u>, HAS MADE HIM <u>KNOWN</u>."

JOHN'S TESTIMONY

USING THE UNDERLINED WORDS BELOW,
FILL IN THE BOXES ON THE NEXT PAGE.

"AND THIS IS THE <u>RECORD</u> OF <u>JOHN</u>, WHEN
THE JEWS SENT <u>PRIESTS</u> AND <u>LEVITES</u> FROM
<u>JERUSALEM</u> TO ASK HIM, WHO ART THOU?"

"AND HE <u>CONFESSED</u>, AND <u>DENIED</u> NOT; BUT
CONFESSED, I AM NOT THE <u>CHRIST</u>."

WHO ARE YOU?

JOHN 1:21–22

USING THE UNDERLINED WORDS BELOW,
FILL IN THE BOXES ON THE NEXT PAGE.

"THEY ASKED HIM, 'THEN <u>WHO</u> ARE YOU? ARE
YOU <u>ELIJAH</u>?'"

"HE SAID, 'I AM NOT.'"

"'ARE YOU THE <u>PROPHET</u>?'"

"HE ANSWERED, 'NO.'"

"FINALLY THEY SAID, 'WHO ARE <u>YOU</u>? GIVE
US AN <u>ANSWER</u> TO TAKE BACK TO THOSE
WHO <u>SENT</u> US. WHAT DO YOU SAY <u>ABOUT</u>
<u>YOURSELF</u>?'"

I AM NOT THE CHRIST

JOHN 1:23–25, KJV

ACROSS

1. "HE SAID, I AM THE _____. "
2. "OF ONE CRYING IN THE _____."
3. "MAKE _____ THE WAY OF THE LORD."
4. "AS SAID THE PROPHET _____."

DOWN

1. "AND THEY WHICH WERE SENT WERE OF THE _____."
2. "AND THEY ASKED HIM, AND SAID UNTO HIM, WHY _____ THOU THEN."
3. "IF THOU BE NOT THAT _____."
4. "NOR ELIAS, NEITHER THAT _____?"

AFTER ME

USING THE UNDERLINED WORDS BELOW,
FILL IN THE BOXES ON THE NEXT PAGE.

"'I <u>BAPTIZE</u> WITH <u>WATER</u>,' JOHN REPLIED,
'BUT <u>AMONG</u> YOU <u>STANDS</u> ONE YOU DO NOT
<u>KNOW</u>.'"

"'HE IS THE ONE <u>WHO</u> COMES AFTER <u>ME</u>,
THE <u>THONGS</u> OF WHOSE <u>SANDALS</u> I AM NOT
<u>WORTHY</u> TO <u>UNTIE</u>.'"

LAMB OF GOD

JOHN 1:29–31, KJV

ACROSS

1. "THE NEXT DAY JOHN SEETH _____ COMING UNTO HIM, AND SAITH."
2. "BEHOLD THE _____ OF GOD."
3. "WHICH TAKETH AWAY THE _____. "
4. "OF THE _____."

DOWN

1. "THIS IS HE OF WHOM I SAID, AFTER ME COMETH A MAN WHICH IS _____ BEFORE ME: FOR HE WAS BEFORE ME. "
2. "AND I _____ HIM NOT."
3. "BUT THAT HE SHOULD BE MADE MANIFEST TO _____."
4. "THEREFORE AM I COME _____ WITH WATER."

23

SON OF GOD

JOHN 1:32–34, KJV

USING THE UNDERLINED WORDS BELOW, FILL IN THE BOXES ON THE NEXT PAGE.

"AND JOHN BARE <u>RECORD</u>, SAYING, I SAW THE SPIRIT DESCENDING FROM <u>HEAVEN</u> LIKE A <u>DOVE</u>, AND IT ABODE UPON HIM. AND I KNEW HIM NOT: BUT HE <u>THAT</u> SENT ME TO <u>BAPTIZE</u> WITH WATER, THE SAME SAID UNTO ME, UPON <u>WHOM</u> THOU SHALT SEE THE <u>SPIRIT</u> DESCENDING, AND <u>REMAINING</u> ON HIM, THE SAME IS HE WHICH BAPTIZETH WITH THE HOLY GHOST. AND I SAW, AND <u>BARE</u> RECORD THAT THIS IS THE <u>SON</u> OF GOD."

25

AT THE JORDAN

JOHN 1:35–36

USING THE UNDERLINED WORDS BELOW, FILL IN THE BOXES ON THE NEXT PAGE.

"THE NEXT DAY <u>JOHN</u> WAS THERE AGAIN WITH TWO OF <u>HIS</u> <u>DISCIPLES</u>."

"WHEN HE SAW <u>JESUS</u> <u>PASSING</u> BY, HE SAID, '<u>LOOK</u>, THE <u>LAMB</u> OF <u>GOD</u>!'"

WATER TO WINE

FROM: JOHN 2:1–6

ACROSS

1. "ON THE THIRD DAY A _____."
2. "TOOK PLACE AT _____ IN GALILEE."
3. "JESUS AND HIS _____ HAD ALSO BEEN INVITED TO THE WEDDING."
4. "WHEN THE WINE WAS GONE, _____' MOTHER SAID TO HIM, 'THEY HAVE NO MORE WINE.'"

DOWN

1. "HIS MOTHER SAID TO THE _____, 'DO WHATEVER HE TELLS YOU.'"
2. "THE KIND USED BY THE JEWS FOR _____ WASHING."
3. "EACH HOLDING FROM _____."
4. "TO THIRTY _____."

29

FILL THE JARS

FROM: JOHN 2:5–9, NKJV

ACROSS

1. "HIS MOTHER SAID TO THE _____."
2. " 'FILL THE WATERPOTS WITH _____.' "
3. "AND THEY FILLED THEM UP TO THE _____."
4. " '_____ SOME OUT NOW.' "

DOWN

1. " 'TAKE IT TO THE _____ OF THE FEAST.' "
2. ANOTHER WORD FOR FEAST.
3. TO UNDERSTAND.
4. "THE SERVANTS WHO HAD _____ THE WATER
   KNEW."

31

THE BRIDEGROOM

FROM: JOHN 2:9–11, NLT

ACROSS

1. "HE CALLED THE _____ OVER."
2. " 'A HOST ALWAYS SERVES THE BEST _____
   FIRST,' HE SAID."
3. SOMETHING THAT IS LESS EXPENSIVE IS

   _____.
4. "THIS _____ SIGN."

DOWN

1. "_____ REVEALED HIS GLORY."
2. "_____ IN GALILEE WAS THE FIRST TIME."
3. "HIS _____."
4. "BELIEVED IN _____."

PASSOVER

FROM: JOHN 2:13–16, NLT

ACROSS

1. "IT WAS NEARLY TIME FOR THE JEWISH _____."
2. "HE SAW MERCHANTS _____ CATTLE."
3. "HE ALSO SAW DEALERS AT _____."
4. "EXCHANGING FOREIGN _____."

DOWN

1. "JESUS MADE A _____ FROM SOME ROPES."
2. "AND CHASED THEM ALL OUT OF THE _____."
3. "GOING OVER TO THE PEOPLE WHO SOLD _____."
4. " 'STOP TURNING MY _____ HOUSE INTO A MARKETPLACE!' "

35

ZEAL FOR MY FATHER'S HOUSE

JOHN 2:17–19, KJV

USING THE UNDERLINED WORDS BELOW, FILL IN THE BOXES ON THE NEXT PAGE.

"AND HIS <u>DISCIPLES</u> REMEMBERED THAT IT WAS WRITTEN, THE <u>ZEAL</u> OF THINE <u>HOUSE</u> HATH <u>EATEN</u> ME UP."

"THEN ANSWERED THE JEWS AND SAID UNTO HIM, WHAT SIGN <u>SWEWEST</u> THOU UNTO US, SEEING THAT THOU DOEST THESE THINGS?"

"JESUS ANSWERED AND SAID UNTO THEM, <u>DESTROY</u> THIS TEMPLE, AND IN THREE DAYS I WILL <u>RAISE</u> IT UP."

NICODEMUS

FROM: JOHN 3:1–3

ACROSS

1. "NOW THERE WAS A MAN OF THE PHARISEES_____."
2. "_____, A MEMBER OF THE JEWISH RULING COUNCIL."
3. "HE CAME TO JESUS AT_____ AND SAID."
4. "'_____, WE KNOW YOU ARE A TEACHER WHO HAS COME FROM GOD.'"

DOWN

1. "'FOR NO ONE COULD _____ THE MIRACULOUS.'"
2. "'_____ YOU ARE DOING IF GOD WERE NOT WITH HIM.'"
3. "'I TELL YOU THE TRUTH, NO ONE CAN SEE THE _____ OF GOD.'
4. "'UNLESS HE IS _____ AGAIN.'"

BORN AGAIN

JOHN 3:4–6, KJV

USING THE UNDERLINED WORDS BELOW, FILL IN THE BOXES ON THE NEXT PAGE.

"<u>NICODEMUS</u> SAITH UNTO HIM, HOW CAN A MAN BE BORN WHEN HE IS <u>OLD</u>? CAN HE ENTER THE <u>SECOND</u> <u>TIME</u> INTO HIS MOTHER'S <u>WOMB</u>, AND BE BORN?"

"JESUS ANSWERED, VERILY, VERILY, I SAY UNTO THEE, EXCEPT A MAN BE BORN OF <u>WATER</u> AND OF THE SPIRIT, HE CANNOT ENTER INTO THE <u>KINGDOM</u> OF GOD."

"THAT WHICH IS BORN OF THE <u>FLESH</u> IS FLESH; AND THAT WHICH IS BORN OF THE SPIRIT IS <u>SPIRIT</u>."

THE WIND BLOWS

FROM: JOHN 3:7–15, NLT

<u>ACROSS</u>

1. "DON'T BE _____ WHEN I SAY, 'YOU MUST BE BORN AGAIN.' "
2. "THE WIND _____ WHEREVER IT WANTS."
3. "YOU CAN _____ THE WIND."
4. "CAN'T TELL WHERE IT _____ FROM."

<u>DOWN</u>

1. "HOW CAN YOU POSSIBLY BELIEVE IF I TELL YOU ABOUT _____ THINGS?"
2. "AS MOSES _____ UP THE BRONZE SNAKE."
3. A SANDY, DRY REGION.
4. "EVERYONE WHO _____ IN HIM WILL HAVE ETERNAL LIFE."

ETERNAL LIFE

JOHN 3:16–17, KJV

USING THE UNDERLINED WORDS BELOW, FILL IN THE BOXES ON THE NEXT PAGE.

"FOR GOD SO <u>LOVED</u> THE WORLD, THAT HE GAVE HIS ONLY BEGOTTEN SON, THAT <u>WHOSOEVER</u> <u>BELIEVETH</u> IN HIM SHOULD NOT PERISH, BUT HAVE <u>EVERLASTING</u> <u>LIFE</u>."

"FOR GOD SENT NOT HIS SON INTO THE WORLD TO <u>CONDEMN</u> THE <u>WORLD</u>; BUT THAT THE WORLD THROUGH HIM MIGHT BE <u>SAVED</u>."

GOD'S ONE AND ONLY SON

JOHN 3:18, KJV

USING THE UNDERLINED WORDS BELOW,
FILL IN THE BOXES ON THE NEXT PAGE.

"HE THAT BELIEVETH ON <u>HIM</u> IS NOT

<u>CONDEMNED</u>: BUT HE <u>THAT</u> BELIEVETH NOT

IS CONDEMNED <u>ALREADY</u>, <u>BECAUSE</u> HE HATH

NOT <u>BELIEVED</u> IN THE <u>NAME</u> OF THE ONLY

<u>BEGOTTEN</u> <u>SON</u> OF GOD."

LIVE BY THE TRUTH

FROM: JOHN 3:19–21, NASB

ACROSS

1. THE DECISION IN A COURT CASE.
2. "MEN LOVED THE _____."
3. "RATHER THAN THE _____."
4. "FOR THEIR _____ WERE EVIL."

DOWN

1. "FOR _____ WHO DOES EVIL HATES THE LIGHT."
2. "HIS DEEDS WILL BE _____."
3. "HE WHO PRACTICES THE _____ COMES TO THE LIGHT."
4. "HAVING BEEN WROUGHT IN _____."

JACOB'S WELL

USING THE UNDERLINED WORDS BELOW, FILL IN THE BOXES ON THE NEXT PAGE.

"AND HE MUST NEEDS GO THROUGH <u>SAMARIA</u>. THEN COMETH HE TO A CITY OF SAMARIA, WHICH IS CALLED <u>SYCHAR</u>, NEAR TO THE PARCEL OF GROUND THAT <u>JACOB</u> GAVE TO HIS <u>SON</u> JOSEPH."

"NOW <u>JACOB'S</u> WELL WAS THERE. <u>JESUS</u> THEREFORE, BEING WEARIED WITH HIS JOURNEY, <u>SAT</u> THUS ON <u>THE</u> WELL: AND IT WAS <u>ABOUT</u> THE <u>SIXTH</u> HOUR."

51

SAMARITAN WOMAN

FROM: JOHN 4:7–12, NKJV

ACROSS

1. A PERSON FROM SAMARIA WAS A _____.
2. "JESUS SAID TO _____, 'GIVE ME A DRINK.' "
3. "THE _____ OF SAMARIA."
4. "HOW IS IT THAT YOU, BEING A JEW, ASK A
   _____ FROM ME, A SAMARITAN WOMAN?"

DOWN

1. " 'IF YOU KNEW THE _____ OF GOD.' "
2. " 'YOU HAVE _____ TO DRAW WITH.' "
3. "JACOB, WHO GAVE US THE WELL, AND _____
   FROM IT HIMSELF."
4. A RANCHER MAY HAVE SEVERAL _____ OF
   CATTLE.

SPRING OF WATER

FROM: JOHN 4:13–22, NCV

ACROSS

1. " 'EVERYONE WHO DRINKS THIS WATER WILL BE
   _____ AGAIN.' "
2. " 'WHOEVER DRINKS THE WATER I GIVE WILL
   _____ BE THIRSTY.' "
3. NOT HER, BUT _____.
4. " 'GIVING _____ LIFE.' "

DOWN

1. " 'BELIEVE ME, _____.' "
2. " '_____ THE FATHER.' "
3. " '_____ COMES.' "
4. " 'FROM THE _____.' "

55

TRUE WORSHIPERS

FROM: JOHN 4:23–26, NLV

ACROSS

1. " 'TRUE _____ WILL WORSHIP.' "
2. " 'THE _____.' "
3. " 'SPIRIT AND IN _____.' "
4. " 'WORSHIP IN _____ AND IN TRUTH.' "

DOWN

1. "THE _____ SAID, 'I KNOW THE MESSIAH IS COMING' "
2. " 'THE ONE WHO IS CALLED _____.' "
3. " 'HE WILL EXPLAIN _____ TO US.' "
4. ANOTHER WORD FOR TALK.

57

57

57

THE WOMAN'S TESTIMONY

FROM: JOHN 4:39–41, NIRV

<u>ACROSS</u>

1. "MANY OF THE _____ FROM THE TOWN OF
   SYCHAR BELIEVED IN JESUS."
2. NOT HER.
3. YOUR WITNESS FOR JESUS CHRIST IS YOUR
   PERSONAL _____.
4. " 'HE TOLD ME _____ I'VE EVER DONE.' "

<u>DOWN</u>

1. "THEN THE SAMARITANS CAME TO HIM AND TRIED
   TO GET HIM TO _____ WITH THEM."
2. "SO HE STAYED TWO _____."
3. "BECAUSE OF HIS _____."
4. "MANY MORE PEOPLE BECAME _____."

59

THE ROYAL OFFICIAL

FROM: JOHN 4:47–49, NCV

ACROSS

1. "JESUS HAD COME FROM JUDEA TO _____."
2. "HE WENT TO JESUS AND _____ HIM."
3. "AND _____ HIS SON."
4. NOT FAR, BUT _____.

DOWN

1. " 'YOU _____ MUST SEE SIGNS AND MIRACLES.' "
2. " 'BEFORE YOU WILL _____ IN ME.' "
3. THE RELATIVES OF A KING OR QUEEN ARE MEMBERS
   OF THE _____ FAMILY.
4. " 'SIR, COME BEFORE MY _____ DIES.' "

61

YOUR SON WILL LIVE

JOHN 4:50–52, KJV

USING THE UNDERLINED WORDS BELOW, FILL IN THE BOXES ON THE NEXT PAGE.

"JESUS SAITH UNTO HIM, GO THY WAY; THY SON LIVETH. AND THE MAN BELIEVED THE WORD THAT JESUS HAD SPOKEN UNTO HIM, AND HE WENT HIS WAY."

"AND AS HE WAS NOW GOING DOWN, HIS SERVANTS MET HIM, AND TOLD HIM, SAYING, THY SON LIVETH."

"THEN INQUIRED HE OF THEM THE HOUR WHEN HE BEGAN TO AMEND. AND THEY SAID UNTO HIM, YESTERDAY AT THE SEVENTH HOUR THE FEVER LEFT HIM."

THE SHEEP GATE

ACROSS

1. "NOW THERE IS IN _____
NEAR THE SHEEP GATE A POOL."
2. "WHICH IN _____ IS CALLED
BETHESDA."
3. "AND WHICH IS _____ BY
FIVE COVERED COLONNADES."
4. "HERE A GREAT NUMBER OF _____
PEOPLE USED TO LIE — THE BLIND, THE LAME,
THE PARALYZED."

DOWN

1. "ONE WHO WAS THERE HAD BEEN AN
_____ FOR THIRTY-EIGHT YEARS."
2. "WHEN JESUS SAW HIM LYING THERE AND
LEARNED THAT HE HAD BEEN IN THIS
_____ FOR A LONG TIME."
3. "HE _____ HIM."
4. "'DO YOU WANT TO GET _____?'"

GET UP

JOHN 5:7–9, KJV

USING THE UNDERLINED WORDS BELOW, FILL IN THE BOXES ON THE NEXT PAGE.

"THE IMPOTENT MAN ANSWERED HIM, SIR, I HAVE NO MAN, WHEN THE <u>WATER</u> IS TROUBLED, TO PUT ME INTO THE <u>POOL</u>: BUT WHILE I AM COMING, ANOTHER <u>STEPPETH</u> DOWN BEFORE ME."

"<u>JESUS</u> SAITH UNTO HIM, RISE, <u>TAKE</u> UP THY BED, AND WALK."

"AND IMMEDIATELY THE MAN WAS MADE <u>WHOLE</u>, AND TOOK UP HIS <u>BED</u>, AND <u>WALKED</u>."

I TELL YOU THE TRUTH

JOHN 5:19-20

ACROSS

1. "JESUS GAVE THEM THIS _____."
2. "'I TELL YOU THE _____.'"
3. "'THE SON CAN DO NOTHING BY _____; HE CAN DO ONLY WHAT HE SEES HIS FATHER DOING.'"
4. "'BECAUSE WHATEVER THE FATHER DOES THE _____ ALSO DOES.'"

DOWN

1. "'FOR THE _____ LOVES THE SON.'"
2. "'AND SHOWS _____ ALL HE DOES.'"
3. "'YES, TO YOUR _____.'"
4. "'HE WILL SHOW HIM EVEN GREATER _____ THAN THESE.'"

THE SON GIVES LIFE

JOHN 5:21–23, KJV

USING THE UNDERLINED WORDS BELOW,
FILL IN THE BOXES ON THE NEXT PAGE.

"FOR AS THE FATHER <u>RAISETH</u> UP THE <u>DEAD</u>,
AND <u>QUICKENETH</u> THEM; EVEN SO THE <u>SON</u>
QUICKENETH WHOM HE WILL."

"FOR THE FATHER <u>JUDGETH</u> NO MAN, BUT
HATH <u>COMMITTED</u> ALL JUDGMENT UNTO THE
SON."

"THAT ALL MEN SHOULD <u>HONOUR</u> THE SON,
EVEN AS THEY HONOUR THE <u>FATHER</u>. HE
THAT HONOURETH NOT THE SON
HONOURETH NOT THE FATHER WHICH <u>HATH</u>
SENT HIM."

DEATH TO LIFE

FROM: JOHN 5:24–27, NLT

ACROSS

1. THE BIBLE IS ALSO CALLED GOD'S _____.
2. A PERSON WHO HAS FAITH IN GOD _____ HIS PROMISES ARE TRUE.
3. " 'HAVE ETERNAL _____.' "
4. " 'THEY WILL NEVER BE _____.' "

DOWN

1. " 'THE _____ WILL HEAR MY VOICE.' "
2. " 'THE FATHER HAS LIFE IN _____.' "
3. " 'HE HAS GIVEN HIM AUTHORITY TO _____ EVERYONE.' "
4. " 'BECAUSE HE IS THE _____ OF MAN.' "

PRAISE FROM GOD

FROM: JOHN 5:41–44, ESV

ACROSS

1. WHEN WE GLORIFY GOD, WE GIVE HIM OUR

    _____.

2. " 'YOU DO NOT HAVE THE _____.' "
3. " '_____ WITHIN YOU.' "
4. " 'I HAVE COME IN MY _____ NAME.' "

DOWN

1. " 'IF ANOTHER COMES IN HIS OWN _____.' "
2. " 'YOU RECEIVE GLORY FROM ONE _____.' "
3. IF YOU TRY REALLY HARD, YOU PUT FORTH A

    GOOD _____.

4. " 'THE GLORY THAT _____ FROM THE ONLY
    GOD.' "

ENOUGH BREAD

JOHN 6:5–7, KJV

USING THE UNDERLINED WORDS BELOW,
FILL IN THE BOXES ON THE NEXT PAGE.

"WHEN <u>JESUS</u> THEN <u>LIFTED</u> UP HIS EYES,
AND SAW A <u>GREAT</u> COMPANY COME UNTO
HIM, HE SAITH UNTO <u>PHILIP</u>, WHENCE
SHALL WE BUY BREAD, THAT THESE MAY
EAT?"

"AND THIS HE SAID TO <u>PROVE</u> <u>HIM</u>: FOR HE
HIMSELF KNEW WHAT HE WOULD DO."

"PHILIP <u>ANSWERED</u> HIM, TWO <u>HUNDRED</u>
PENNYWORTH OF <u>BREAD</u> IS NOT SUFFICIENT
FOR THEM, THAT EVERY ONE OF THEM MAY
<u>TAKE</u> A <u>LITTLE</u>."

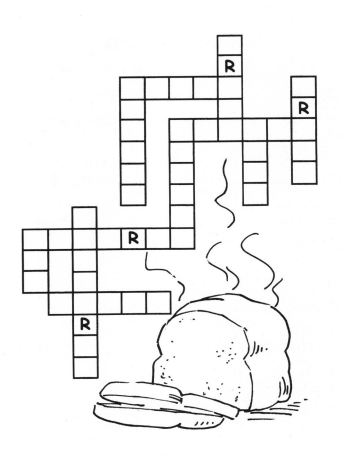

GIVING THANKS

FROM: JOHN 6:10–13, NKJV

ACROSS

1. "THEN JESUS SAID, MAKE THE PEOPLE SIT
   _____.' "
2. "THERE WAS MUCH _____ IN THE PLACE."
3. "SO THE MEN SAT DOWN, IN NUMBER ABOUT FIVE
   _____."
4. "WHEN HE HAD GIVEN _____ HE DISTRIBUTED
   THEM."

DOWN

1. "HE SAID TO HIS _____, 'GATHER UP THE
   FRAGMENTS THAT REMAIN.' "
2. IF SOMETHING IS USED UP CARELESSLY, IT IS

   _____.
3. "FIVE BARLEY _____."
4. "LEFT OVER BY THOSE WHO HAD _____."

A STRONG WIND

FROM: JOHN 6:16–21, ESV

ACROSS

1. "WHEN _____ CAME, HIS DISCIPLES WENT DOWN TO THE SEA."
2. "GOT INTO A _____."
3. "IT WAS NOW _____."
4. "A STRONG _____ WAS BLOWING."

DOWN

1. "THEY HAD ROWED ABOUT _____ OR FOUR MILES."
2. "THEY SAW JESUS _____ ON THE SEA."
3. ANOTHER WORD FOR FRIGHTENED.
4. " 'IT IS I; DO NOT BE _____.' "

81

FOOD THAT SPOILS

JOHN 6:26–27, KJV

USING THE UNDERLINED WORDS BELOW,
FILL IN THE BOXES ON THE NEXT PAGE.

"JESUS ANSWERED THEM AND SAID, <u>VERILY</u>,
VERILY, I SAY UNTO YOU, YE <u>SEEK</u> ME, NOT
<u>BECAUSE</u> YE SAW THE <u>MIRACLES</u>, BUT
BECAUSE YE DID EAT OF THE <u>LOAVES</u>, AND
WERE FILLED."

"<u>LABOUR</u> NOT FOR THE MEAT WHICH
PERISHETH, BUT FOR THAT MEAT WHICH
<u>ENDURETH</u> UNTO <u>EVERLASTING</u> LIFE, WHICH
THE SON OF MAN SHALL GIVE UNTO YOU:
FOR HIM <u>HATH</u> GOD <u>THE</u> FATHER <u>SEALED</u>."

BREAD OF LIFE

JOHN 6:35–37, KJV

USING THE UNDERLINED WORDS BELOW,
FILL IN THE BOXES ON THE NEXT PAGE.

"AND <u>JESUS</u> SAID UNTO THEM, I AM THE
<u>BREAD</u> OF LIFE: HE THAT COMETH TO ME
SHALL <u>NEVER</u> HUNGER; AND HE THAT
BELIEVETH ON ME SHALL NEVER <u>THIRST</u>."

"BUT I SAID UNTO YOU, THAT YE ALSO <u>HAVE</u>
<u>SEEN</u> ME, AND <u>BELIEVE</u> NOT."

"ALL THAT THE <u>FATHER</u> GIVETH ME SHALL
<u>COME</u> TO ME; AND HIM THAT <u>COMETH</u> TO ME
I WILL IN NO WISE CAST OUT."

85

FROM HEAVEN

JOHN 6:38–40, KJV

USING THE UNDERLINED WORDS BELOW, FILL IN THE BOXES ON THE NEXT PAGE.

"FOR I CAME DOWN FROM <u>HEAVEN</u>, NOT TO DO MINE OWN WILL, BUT THE <u>WILL</u> OF HIM THAT SENT ME."

"AND THIS IS THE <u>FATHER'S</u> WILL WHICH HATH <u>SENT</u> <u>ME</u>, THAT OF ALL WHICH HE HATH GIVEN ME I SHOULD <u>LOSE</u> NOTHING, BUT SHOULD <u>RAISE</u> IT UP AGAIN AT THE LAST DAY."

"AND THIS IS THE WILL OF HIM THAT SENT ME, THAT EVERY ONE WHICH SEETH THE SON, AND BELIEVETH ON HIM, MAY HAVE <u>EVERLASTING</u> <u>LIFE</u>: AND I WILL RAISE HIM UP AT THE <u>LAST</u> DAY."

THE SPIRIT GIVES LIFE

FROM: JOHN 6:63–65, NASB

ACROSS

1. " 'IT IS THE SPIRIT WHO GIVES _____.' "
2. " 'THE _____ PROFITS NOTHING.' "
3. " 'THE _____ THAT I HAVE SPOKEN TO YOU ARE
   SPIRIT AND ARE LIFE.' "
4. THE PLURAL OF HE, SHE, OR IT.

DOWN

1. IF AN IDEA IS UNDERSTOOD, IT IS _____.
2. "WHO IT WAS THAT WOULD _____ HIM."
3. " 'FOR _____ REASON I HAVE SAID TO YOU,
   THAT NO ONE CAN COME TO ME UNLESS IT HAS
   BEEN GRANTED HIM FROM THE FATHER.' "
4. TO GIVE THE ABILITY TO DO SOMETHING.

THE FEAST

FROM: JOHN 7:6–15, ESV

ACROSS

1. " 'MY _____ HAS NOT YET COME.' "
2. " 'THE WORLD CANNOT _____ YOU.' "
3. " 'YOU GO UP TO THE _____.' "
4. "THE _____ WERE LOOKING FOR HIM AT THE FEAST."

DOWN

1. IF NEWS IS KNOWN THROUGHOUT A REGION, IT IS _____.
2. "FOR _____ OF THE JEWS NO ONE SPOKE OPENLY OF HIM."
3. "JESUS WENT UP INTO THE _____ AND BEGAN TEACHING."
4. " 'HOW IS IT THAT THIS MAN HAS LEARNING, WHEN HE HAS NEVER _____?' "

91

DOING GOD'S WILL

FROM: JOHN 7:16–18, NCV

<u>ACROSS</u>

1. " 'JESUS _____, "THE THINGS I TEACH ARE NOT MY OWN.' "
2. " 'THEY COME FROM HIM WHO _____ ME.' "
3. " 'THEY _____ KNOW.' "
4. " 'MY _____ COMES FROM GOD.' "

<u>DOWN</u>

1. A SYNONYM FOR TALKS.
2. THOSE WHO TEACH THEIR OWN IDEAS ARE TRYING TO GET _____ FOR THEMSELVES.
3. " 'THE ONE WHO SENT THEM SPEAK THE _____.' "
4. " 'THERE IS NOTHING _____ IN THEM.' "

THE GREATEST DAY

FROM: JOHN 7:37–39, NASB

<u>ACROSS</u>

1. NOT THE LEAST, BUT THE _____.
2. " 'IF ANYONE IS _____.' "
3. " 'LET HIM COME TO ME AND _____.' "
4. " 'HE WHO _____ IN ME.' "

<u>DOWN</u>

1. " 'RIVERS OF LIVING _____.' "
2. NOT WITHOUT, BUT _____.
3. "THIS HE SPOKE OF THE _____."
4. "JESUS WAS NOT YET _____."

95

LIGHT OF LIFE

FROM: JOHN 8:12–18, ESV

ACROSS

1. " 'I AM THE _____ OF THE WORLD.' "
2. " 'WHOEVER FOLLOWS ME WILL NOT WALK IN _____.' "
3. IF SOMEONE CANNOT SPEAK AND YOU SPEAK FOR HIM, YOU ARE SPEAKING ON HIS _____.
4. WHEN YOU THINK HARD ENOUGH, YOU MAY JUST COME UP WITH A GREAT _____.

DOWN

1. " 'MY _____ IS TRUE.' "
2. " 'IT IS NOT I _____ WHO JUDGE.' "
3. " 'THE _____ OF TWO PEOPLE IS TRUE.' "
4. " 'THE FATHER WHO SENT ME BEARS _____ ABOUT ME.' "

97

THE WORLD

JOHN 8:23–24, KJV

USING THE UNDERLINED WORDS BELOW, FILL IN THE BOXES ON THE NEXT PAGE.

"AND HE SAID UNTO THEM, YE ARE FROM <u>BENEATH</u>; I AM FROM <u>ABOVE</u>: YE ARE OF THIS <u>WORLD</u>; I AM <u>NOT</u> OF THIS WORLD."

"I SAID <u>THEREFORE</u> UNTO YOU, THAT YE SHALL <u>DIE</u> IN YOUR <u>SINS</u>: FOR IF YE <u>BELIEVE</u> NOT THAT I AM HE, YE SHALL <u>DIE</u> IN YOUR SINS."

FREE INDEED

JOHN 8:34–36, KJV

USING THE UNDERLINED WORDS BELOW,
FILL IN THE BOXES ON THE NEXT PAGE.

"JESUS ANSWERED THEM, <u>VERILY</u>, VERILY, I
SAY <u>UNTO</u> YOU, <u>WHOSOEVER</u> <u>COMMITTETH</u>
SIN IS THE SERVANT OF <u>SIN</u>."

"AND THE <u>SERVANT</u> ABIDETH NOT IN THE
<u>HOUSE</u> FOR EVER: BUT THE SON ABIDETH
EVER. "

"IF THE <u>SON</u> THEREFORE SHALL MAKE YOU
FREE, YE SHALL BE <u>FREE</u> INDEED."

101

HEAR WHAT I SAY

FROM: JOHN 8:42–47, NCV

ACROSS

1. " 'IF GOD WERE REALLY YOUR _____, YOU
   WOULD LOVE ME.' "
2. " 'I DID NOT COME BY MY _____ AUTHORITY.' "
3. ENGLISH IS ONE, AS WELL AS SPANISH OR
   FRENCH.
4. " 'YOU BELONG TO YOUR FATHER THE _____.' "

DOWN

1. EARLY RESIDENTS OF NORTH AMERICA WERE
   _____ AMERICANS.
2. " 'HE IS A _____ AND THE FATHER OF LIES.' "
3. " 'CAN ANY OF YOU PROVE THAT I AM _____ OF
   SIN?' "
4. " 'YOU DON'T _____ TO GOD.' "

103

I AM THE GATE

FROM: JOHN 10:7–10

ACROSS

1. "_____ JESUS SAID AGAIN, 'I TELL YOU THE TRUTH.'"
2. "'I AM THE _____ FOR THE SHEEP.'"
3. "'ALL WHO EVER CAME BEFORE ME WERE _____ AND ROBBERS.'"
4. "'BUT THE SHEEP DID NOT _____ TO THEM.'"

DOWN

1. "'HE WILL COME IN AND GO OUT, AND FIND _____.'"
2. "'THE THIEF COMES ONLY TO _____.'"
3. "'I HAVE COME THAT THEY MAY HAVE _____.'"
4. "'AND HAVE IT TO THE _____.'"

105

THE GOOD SHEPHERD

FROM: JOHN 10:14–18, NLT

ACROSS

1. " 'I AM THE GOOD _____.' "
2. " 'I KNOW MY OWN _____.' "
3. " 'I KNOW THE _____.' "
4. " 'THEY WILL _____ TO MY VOICE.' "

DOWN

1. " 'THE FATHER _____ ME.' "
2. " 'TAKE IT _____ AGAIN.' "
3. NOT GIVES, BUT _____.
4. HE GAVE THE GIFT, AND I _____ IT.

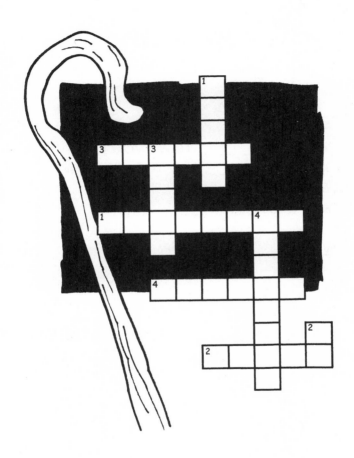

MY SHEEP

FROM: JOHN 10:27–29, NLT

ACROSS

1. " 'MY SHEEP _____ TO MY VOICE.' "
2. " 'I KNOW _____, AND THEY FOLLOW ME.' "
3. " 'I GIVE THEM _____ LIFE.' "
4. " 'THEY WILL NEVER _____.' "

DOWN

1. NOT IN.
2. " 'MY FATHER HAS GIVEN THEM TO ME.' "
3. _____ THAN, LESS THAN, OR EQUAL TO?
4. " 'NO ONE CAN _____ THEM FROM THE FATHER'S HAND.' "

109

LAZARUS

FROM: JOHN 11:1–6, NASB

ACROSS

1. "NOW A CERTAIN MAN WAS SICK, _____ OF BETHANY."
2. "THE VILLAGE OF _____ AND HER SISTER MARTHA."
3. "IT WAS THE MARY WHO. . .WIPED HIS FEET WITH HER _____."
4. " '_____, BEHOLD, HE WHOM YOU LOVE IS SICK.' "

DOWN

1. "BUT WHEN JESUS _____ THIS, HE SAID, 'THIS SICKNESS IS NOT TO END IN DEATH.' "
2. " 'BUT FOR THE _____ OF GOD.' "
3. "NOW JESUS LOVED _____ AND HER SISTER AND LAZARUS."
4. "HE THEN _____ TWO DAYS LONGER IN THE PLACE WHERE HE WAS."

HE IS DEAD

FROM: JOHN 11:11–15, NIRV

<u>ACROSS</u>

1. "AFTER HE _____ THIS, JESUS WENT ON
   SPEAKING TO THEM."
2. " 'OUR _____ LAZARUS HAS FALLEN ASLEEP.' "
3. " 'BUT I AM GOING THERE TO _____ HIM UP.' "
4. ANOTHER WORD FOR SLUMBERS.

<u>DOWN</u>

1. TALKING, OR _____.
2. "HIS _____ THOUGHT HE MEANT NATURAL
   SLEEP."
3. "SO THEN HE TOLD THEM PLAINLY, 'LAZARUS IS
   DEAD.' "
4. FOR YOUR BENEFIT, OR FOR YOUR _____.

113

HE WILL RISE

FROM: JOHN 11:17–24, ESV

ACROSS

1. WHEN JESUS ENTERED A TOWN, IT CAN ALSO BE SAID THAT IT WAS HIS _____.
2. "_____ WAS NEAR JERUSALEM."
3. MANY WHO _____ JESUS' WORDS BELIEVED IN HIM.
4. "_____ REMAINED SEATED IN THE HOUSE."

DOWN

1. " 'LORD, IF YOU HAD _____ HERE, MY BROTHER WOULD NOT HAVE DIED.' "
2. " 'I KNOW THAT WHATEVER YOU _____ FROM GOD, GOD WILL GIVE YOU.' "
3. "JESUS SAID TO HER, 'YOUR BROTHER WILL RISE _____.' "
4. " 'I KNOW THAT HE WILL RISE AGAIN IN THE _____ ON THE LAST DAY.' "

115

I BELIEVE

JOHN 11:25–27, KJV

USING THE UNDERLINED WORDS BELOW, FILL IN THE BOXES ON THE NEXT PAGE.

"JESUS SAID UNTO HER, I AM THE RESURRECTION, AND THE LIFE: HE THAT BELIEVETH IN ME, THOUGH HE WERE DEAD, YET SHALL HE LIVE."

"AND WHOSOEVER LIVETH AND BELIEVETH IN ME SHALL NEVER DIE. BELIEVEST THOU THIS?"

"SHE SAITH UNTO HIM, YEA, LORD: I BELIEVE THAT THOU ART THE CHRIST, THE SON OF GOD, WHICH SHOULD COME INTO THE WORLD."

MARY WEEPS

FROM: JOHN 11:32-39, NASB

<u>ACROSS</u>

1. WHEN YOU HAVE ARRIVED, YOU HAVE _____ YOUR DESTINATION.
2. "HE WAS DEEPLY MOVED IN _____ AND WAS TROUBLED."
3. " 'WHERE HAVE YOU _____ HIM?' "
4. "JESUS _____."

<u>DOWN</u>

1. "JESUS, AGAIN BEING _____ MOVED WITHIN, CAME TO THE TOMB."
2. "IT WAS A CAVE, AND A _____ WAS LYING AGAINST IT."
3. " '_____, BY THIS TIME THERE WILL BE A STENCH.' "
4. " 'HE HAS BEEN _____ FOUR DAYS.' "

119

COME OUT

FROM: JOHN 11:41–44, NLT

ACROSS

1. "SO THEY ROLLED THE _____ ASIDE."
2. " '_____, THANK YOU FOR HEARING ME.' "
3. " 'YOU ALWAYS _____ ME.' "
4. " 'I SAID IT. . .SO THAT THEY WILL BELIEVE
   _____ SENT ME.' "

DOWN

1. "THEN _____ SHOUTED, 'LAZARUS, COME OUT!' "
2. "THE _____ MAN CAME OUT."
3. "HIS FACE _____ IN A HEADCLOTH."
4. AT THE START OF EACH DAY, YOU PUT ON YOUR

   _____.

LORD AND TEACHER

FROM: JOHN 13:12–16, NCV

1. "HE HAD _____ WASHING THEIR FEET."
2. " 'DO YOU _____ WHAT I HAVE JUST DONE FOR YOU?' "
3. "YOU CALL ME '_____.' "
4. " 'I. . .HAVE _____ YOUR FEET.' "

1. GET READY, GET _____. . .
2. " 'I TELL YOU THE _____.' "
3. " 'A _____ IS NOT GREATER THAN HIS MASTER.' "
4. " 'A _____ IS NOT GREATER THAN THE ONE WHO SENT HIM.' "

123

ONE WILL BETRAY ME

JOHN 13:21, 26–27, KJV

USING THE UNDERLINED WORDS BELOW,
FILL IN THE BOXES ON THE NEXT PAGE.

"WHEN JESUS HAD THUS SAID, HE WAS
TROUBLED IN SPIRIT, AND TESTIFIED, AND
SAID, VERILY, VERILY, I SAY UNTO YOU,
THAT ONE OF YOU SHALL BETRAY ME."

"JESUS ANSWERED, HE IT IS, TO WHOM I
SHALL GIVE A SOP, WHEN I HAVE DIPPED IT.
AND WHEN HE HAD DIPPED THE SOP, HE
GAVE IT TO JUDAS ISCARIOT, THE SON OF
SIMON."

"AND AFTER THE SOP SATAN ENTERED INTO
HIM."

125

A NEW COMMAND

FROM: JOHN 13:34–35, 14:1–3, ESV

<u>ACROSS</u>

1. " 'A _____ COMMANDMENT I GIVE TO YOU;' "
2. " '_____ ONE ANOTHER.' "
3. " 'YOU ALSO ARE TO LOVE ONE _____.' "
4. " 'ALL PEOPLE WILL KNOW THAT YOU ARE MY
   _____.' "

<u>DOWN</u>

1. " 'LET NOT YOUR _____ BE TROUBLED.' "
2. " 'IN MY FATHER'S HOUSE ARE MANY _____.' "
3. " 'I GO TO PREPARE A _____ FOR YOU.' "
4. " 'IF I GO AND _____ A PLACE FOR YOU, I WILL
   COME AGAIN AND WILL TAKE YOU TO MYSELF.' "

THE COUNSELOR

USING THE UNDERLINED WORDS BELOW, FILL IN THE BOXES ON THE NEXT PAGE.

"IF YE LOVE ME, KEEP MY <u>COMMANDMENTS</u>."

"AND I WILL PRAY THE FATHER, AND HE SHALL <u>GIVE</u> YOU ANOTHER <u>COMFORTER</u>, THAT HE MAY ABIDE WITH YOU FOR EVER; EVEN THE <u>SPIRIT</u> OF TRUTH; WHOM THE <u>WORLD</u> CANNOT RECEIVE, BECAUSE IT SEETH HIM NOT, NEITHER <u>KNOWETH</u> HIM: BUT YE KNOW HIM; FOR HE DWELLETH WITH YOU, AND SHALL BE IN YOU."

"I WILL <u>NOT</u> LEAVE YOU <u>COMFORTLESS</u>: I WILL <u>COME</u> TO YOU."

129

OBEY MY TEACHINGS

JOHN 14:23–24, KJV

USING THE UNDERLINED WORDS BELOW,
FILL IN THE BOXES ON THE NEXT PAGE.

"JESUS ANSWERED AND <u>SAID</u> UNTO HIM, IF
A MAN LOVE ME, HE WILL KEEP MY WORDS:
AND MY <u>FATHER</u> WILL LOVE HIM, AND WE
WILL COME UNTO <u>HIM</u>, AND MAKE OUR
<u>ABODE</u> WITH HIM."

"HE THAT LOVETH ME NOT <u>KEEPETH</u> NOT MY
<u>SAYINGS</u>: AND THE WORD WHICH YE <u>HEAR</u>
IS <u>NOT</u> MINE, BUT THE FATHER'S <u>WHICH</u>
<u>SENT</u> ME."

131

THE HOLY SPIRIT

FROM: JOHN 14:25–31, NCV

ACROSS

1. WORDS THAT HAVE BEEN SAID HAVE BEEN
   _____.

2. " 'THIS HELPER IS THE HOLY SPIRIT WHOM THE
   FATHER WILL SEND IN MY _____.' "

3. " 'I LEAVE YOU _____.' "

4. " 'SO DON'T LET YOUR _____ BE TROUBLED OR
   AFRAID.' "

DOWN

1. " 'YOU _____ ME SAY TO YOU, "I AM GOING,
   BUT I AM COMING BACK TO YOU." ' "

2. " 'I HAVE TOLD YOU THIS NOW, BEFORE IT
   _____.' "

3. " 'THE WORLD MUST KNOW THAT I LOVE THE
   _____.' "

4. LET'S GO, IT'S TIME TO _____.

133

I AM THE VINE

FROM: JOHN 15:1–6, NASB

<u>ACROSS</u>

1. " 'I AM THE TRUE _____.' "
2. " 'EVERY BRANCH IN ME THAT DOES NOT BEAR FRUIT. . .HE _____.' "
3. " 'YOU ARE ALREADY _____ BECAUSE OF THE WORD WHICH I HAVE SPOKEN TO YOU.' "
4. " 'AS THE _____ CANNOT BEAR FRUIT OF ITSELF.' "

<u>DOWN</u>

1. " 'I AM THE VINE, YOU ARE THE _____.' "
2. TO STAY BEHIND WHILE OTHERS GO ON AHEAD.
3. " 'IF ANYONE DOES NOT ABIDE IN ME, HE IS _____ AWAY.' "
4. A FLOWER THAT DIES DRIES UP AND _____.

135

I LOVE YOU

FROM: JOHN 15:9–16

ACROSS

1. "'AS THE FATHER HAS _____ ME, SO HAVE I LOVED YOU.'"
2. "'NOW _____ IN MY LOVE.'"
3. "'IF YOU OBEY MY _____, YOU WILL REMAIN IN MY LOVE.'"
4. "'JUST AS I HAVE _____ MY FATHER'S COMMANDS AND REMAIN IN HIS LOVE.'"

DOWN

1. "'_____ LOVE HAS NO ONE THAN THIS.'"
2. "'THAT HE LAY DOWN HIS LIFE FOR HIS _____.'"
3. "'BECAUSE A SERVANT DOES NOT KNOW HIS _____ BUSINESS.'"
4. "'YOU DID NOT _____ ME, BUT I CHOSE YOU.'"

137

I HAVE CHOSEN YOU

FROM: JOHN 15:18–25

ACROSS

1. "'IF THE _____ HATES YOU, KEEP IN MIND THAT IT HATED ME FIRST.'"
2. "'IF YOU _____ TO THE WORLD, IT WOULD LOVE YOU AS ITS OWN.'"
3. "'THAT IS WHY THE WORLD _____ YOU.'"
4. "'NO SERVANT IS GREATER THAN HIS _____.'"

DOWN

1. "'THEY WILL _____ YOU THIS WAY BECAUSE OF MY NAME.'"
2. "'HE WHO HATES ME HATES MY _____ AS WELL.'"
3. "'THEY WOULD NOT BE _____ OF SIN.'"
4. "'THEY HATED ME WITHOUT _____.'"

THE COUNSELOR

JOHN 16:5–11, KJV

USING THE UNDERLINED WORDS BELOW, FILL IN THE BOXES ON THE NEXT PAGE.

"BUT NOW I GO MY WAY TO HIM THAT <u>SENT</u> ME; AND <u>NONE</u> OF YOU ASKETH ME, WHITHER GOEST THOU? BUT BECAUSE I HAVE SAID THESE THINGS UNTO YOU, <u>SORROW</u> HATH FILLED YOUR HEART."

"NEVERTHELESS I TELL YOU THE <u>TRUTH</u>; IT IS EXPEDIENT FOR YOU THAT I GO <u>AWAY</u>: FOR IF I GO NOT AWAY, THE <u>COMFORTER</u> WILL NOT COME UNTO YOU; BUT IF I <u>DEPART</u>, I WILL SEND HIM UNTO YOU."

"AND <u>WHEN</u> HE IS COME, HE WILL REPROVE THE WORLD OF SIN, AND OF RIGHTEOUSNESS, AND OF JUDGMENT: OF SIN, BECAUSE THEY BELIEVE NOT ON ME; OF RIGHTEOUSNESS, BECAUSE I GO TO MY FATHER, AND YE SEE ME <u>NO</u> MORE; OF JUDGMENT, BECAUSE THE <u>PRINCE</u> OF THIS WORLD IS <u>JUDGED</u>."

GLORIFY YOUR SON

JOHN 17:1–5, KJV

USING THE UNDERLINED WORDS BELOW, FILL IN THE BOXES ON THE NEXT PAGE.

"THESE <u>WORDS</u> SPAKE JESUS, AND LIFTED UP HIS EYES TO <u>HEAVEN</u>, AND SAID, FATHER, THE HOUR IS COME; GLORIFY THY <u>SON</u>, THAT THY SON ALSO MAY GLORIFY THEE: AS THOU HAST GIVEN HIM POWER OVER ALL FLESH, THAT HE SHOULD GIVE ETERNAL <u>LIFE</u> TO AS MANY AS THOU HAST GIVEN HIM."

"AND THIS IS LIFE <u>ETERNAL</u>, THAT THEY MIGHT KNOW THEE THE ONLY <u>TRUE</u> GOD, AND JESUS CHRIST, WHOM THOU HAST SENT."

"I HAVE GLORIFIED THEE ON THE EARTH: I HAVE <u>FINISHED</u> THE WORK WHICH THOU GAVEST ME TO DO. AND NOW, O <u>FATHER</u>, <u>GLORIFY</u> THOU ME WITH THINE OWN SELF WITH THE GLORY WHICH I HAD WITH THEE BEFORE THE <u>WORLD</u> WAS."

THEY BELIEVED

FROM: JOHN 17:6–12

ACROSS

1. "'I HAVE _____ YOU TO THOSE WHOM YOU GAVE ME OUT OF THE WORLD.'"
2. "'YOU GAVE THEM TO ME AND THEY HAVE _____ YOUR WORD.'"
3. "'I AM NOT PRAYING FOR THE WORLD, BUT FOR THOSE YOU HAVE _____ ME.'"
4. "'FOR THEY ARE _____.'"

DOWN

1. "'I WILL REMAIN IN THE WORLD NO _____.'"
2. "'PROTECT THEM BY THE POWER OF YOUR NAME—THE _____ YOU GAVE ME.'"
3. "'_____ HAS BEEN LOST EXCEPT THE ONE DOOMED TO DESTRUCTION.'"
4. "'SO THAT SCRIPTURE WOULD BE _____.'"

145

SANCTIFIED

FROM: JOHN 17:13–19, NASB

1. " 'THESE _____ I SPEAK IN THE WORLD.' "
2. WHAT YOU DO WITH A RULER.
3. " 'I HAVE GIVEN THEM YOUR _____.' "
4. " 'KEEP THEM FROM THE _____ ONE.' "

DOWN

1. " 'THEY ARE NOT OF THE _____.' "
2. " 'AS YOU _____ ME INTO THE WORLD, I ALSO HAVE SENT THEM INTO THE WORLD.' "
3. " 'FOR THEIR SAKES I SANCTIFY _____.' "
4. " 'THAT THEY THEMSELVES ALSO MAY BE _____ IN TRUTH.' "

147

RIGHTEOUS FATHER

JOHN 17:24–26, KJV

USING THE UNDERLINED WORDS BELOW,
FILL IN THE BOXES ON THE NEXT PAGE.

"FATHER, I WILL THAT THEY ALSO, WHOM
THOU HAST GIVEN ME, BE WITH ME WHERE
I AM; THAT THEY MAY BEHOLD MY GLORY,
WHICH THOU HAST GIVEN ME: FOR THOU
LOVEDST ME BEFORE THE FOUNDATION OF
THE WORLD."

"O RIGHTEOUS FATHER, THE WORLD HATH
NOT KNOWN THEE: BUT I HAVE KNOWN
THEE, AND THESE HAVE KNOWN THAT THOU
HAST SENT ME."

"AND I HAVE DECLARED UNTO THEM THY
NAME, AND WILL DECLARE IT: THAT THE
LOVE WHEREWITH THOU HAST LOVED ME
MAY BE IN THEM, AND I IN THEM."

JESUS OF NAZARETH

FROM: JOHN 18:4–11, ESV

ACROSS

1. "JESUS, KNOWING ALL THAT WOULD _____ TO HIM, CAME FORWARD AND SAID TO THEM, 'WHOM DO YOU SEEK?' "
2. "THEY ANSWERED HIM, 'JESUS OF _____.' "
3. "THEY DREW BACK AND FELL TO THE _____."
4. "THEY SAID, '_____ OF NAZARETH.' "

DOWN

1. "THIS WAS TO FULFILL THE WORD THAT HE HAD _____."
2. "SIMON PETER, HAVING A _____, DREW IT AND STRUCK THE HIGH PRIEST'S SERVANT."
3. ANOTHER WORD FOR ORDERED.
4. " 'SHALL I NOT _____ THE CUP THAT THE FATHER HAS GIVEN ME?' "

151

JESUS ARRESTED

FROM: JOHN 18:12–16

ACROSS

1. "THEN THE _____ OF SOLDIERS
   WITH ITS COMMANDER AND THE JEWISH
   OFFICIALS ARRESTED JESUS."
2. "ANNAS, WHO WAS THE FATHER-IN-LAW OF
   _____."
3. "THE HIGH _____ THAT YEAR."
4. "IT WOULD BE GOOD IF ONE MAN _____
   FOR THE PEOPLE."

DOWN

1. "HE WENT WITH JESUS INTO THE HIGH
   PRIEST'S _____."
2. "THE OTHER _____, WHO WAS
   KNOWN TO THE HIGH PRIEST."
3. "CAME BACK, SPOKE TO THE GIRL ON
   _____ THERE."
4. "AND BROUGHT _____ IN."

153

QUESTIONING JESUS

FROM: JOHN 18:19–26, NASB

<u>ACROSS</u>

1. "THE HIGH PRIEST THEN QUESTIONED JESUS ABOUT HIS DISCIPLES, AND ABOUT HIS _____."
2. " 'I HAVE SPOKEN OPENLY TO THE WORLD; I ALWAYS TAUGHT IN SYNAGOGUES AND IN THE _____.' "
3. " 'I SPOKE NOTHING IN _____.' "
4. " 'IS THAT THE WAY YOU ANSWER THE HIGH _____?' "

<u>DOWN</u>

1. " 'IF I HAVE SPOKEN WRONGLY, TESTIFY OF THE WRONG.' "
2. A PERSON WHO TELLS NO LIES SPEAKS ONLY THE _____.
3. "ONE OF THE SLAVES OF THE HIGH PRIEST, BEING A _____."
4. "ONE WHOSE _____ PETER CUT OFF, SAID, 'DID I NOT SEE YOU IN THE GARDEN WITH HIM?' "

155

NO POWER

JOHN 19:11–15, KJV

USING THE UNDERLINED WORDS BELOW, FILL IN THE BOXES ON THE NEXT PAGE.

"JESUS ANSWERED, THOU COULDEST HAVE NO <u>POWER</u> AT ALL AGAINST ME, EXCEPT IT WERE GIVEN THEE FROM <u>ABOVE</u>: THEREFORE HE THAT DELIVERED ME UNTO THEE HATH THE <u>GREATER</u> SIN."

"AND FROM THENCEFORTH <u>PILATE</u> SOUGHT TO RELEASE HIM: BUT THE JEWS CRIED OUT, SAYING, IF THOU LET THIS MAN GO, THOU ART NOT CAESAR'S FRIEND: WHOSOEVER MAKETH HIMSELF A KING SPEAKETH AGAINST <u>CAESAR</u>. "

"WHEN PILATE THEREFORE <u>HEARD</u> THAT SAYING, HE BROUGHT JESUS FORTH, AND SAT DOWN IN THE JUDGMENT SEAT IN A PLACE THAT IS <u>CALLED</u> THE PAVEMENT, BUT IN THE HEBREW, GABBATHA. AND IT WAS THE PREPARATION OF THE <u>PASSOVER</u>, AND ABOUT THE SIXTH HOUR: AND HE SAITH UNTO THE JEWS, BEHOLD YOUR KING!"

"BUT THEY CRIED OUT, <u>AWAY</u> WITH HIM, AWAY WITH HIM, <u>CRUCIFY</u> HIM."

THE CROSS

USING THE UNDERLINED WORDS BELOW,
FILL IN THE BOXES ON THE NEXT PAGE.

"THEN <u>DELIVERED</u> HE HIM THEREFORE UNTO
THEM TO BE <u>CRUCIFIED</u>. AND THEY TOOK
JESUS, AND <u>LED</u> HIM AWAY."

"AND HE <u>BEARING</u> HIS CROSS WENT FORTH
INTO A PLACE CALLED THE <u>PLACE</u> OF A SKULL,
WHICH IS <u>CALLED</u> IN THE HEBREW
GOLGOTHA:"

"<u>WHERE</u> THEY CRUCIFIED HIM, AND <u>TWO</u>
OTHERS WITH HIM, ON <u>EITHER</u> <u>SIDE</u> ONE,
AND JESUS IN THE <u>MIDST</u>."

IT IS FINISHED

JOHN 19:28–30, KJV

USING THE UNDERLINED WORDS BELOW, FILL IN THE BOXES ON THE NEXT PAGE.

"AFTER THIS, JESUS KNOWING <u>THAT</u> ALL THINGS WERE NOW <u>ACCOMPLISHED</u>, THAT THE SCRIPTURE MIGHT BE FULFILLED, SAITH, I <u>THIRST</u>."

"NOW THERE WAS SET A VESSEL FULL OF <u>VINEGAR</u>: AND THEY FILLED A <u>SPONGE</u> WITH VINEGAR, AND PUT IT UPON HYSSOP, AND PUT IT TO <u>HIS</u> MOUTH."

"WHEN JESUS THEREFORE HAD <u>RECEIVED</u> THE VINEGAR, HE <u>SAID</u>, IT IS <u>FINISHED</u>: AND HE BOWED HIS HEAD, AND GAVE UP THE GHOST."

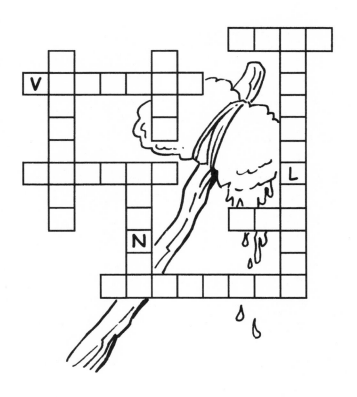

THE TOMB IS EMPTY

FROM: JOHN 20:3–9, ESV

<u>ACROSS</u>

1. "SO PETER WENT OUT WITH THE OTHER DISCIPLE, AND THEY WERE GOING TOWARD THE _____."
2. "BOTH OF THEM WERE _____ TOGETHER."
3. "HE SAW THE _____ CLOTHS LYING THERE."
4. "THEN _____ PETER CAME, FOLLOWING HIM, AND WENT INTO THE TOMB."

<u>DOWN</u>

1. "HE SAW THE LINEN CLOTHS LYING THERE, AND THE FACE _____."
2. WHEN PETER ARRIVED AT THE TOMB, HE WENT _____.
3. "THEN THE OTHER DISCIPLE. . .SAW AND _____."
4. "FOR AS YET THEY DID NOT UNDERSTAND THE _____, THAT HE MUST RISE FROM THE DEAD."

MY LORD

FROM: JOHN 20:10–14, NKJV

<u>ACROSS</u>

1. "THEN THE DISCIPLES WENT AWAY AGAIN TO THEIR OWN _____."
2. MARY WAS WEEPING, OR _____.
3. "SHE SAW TWO _____ IN WHITE."
4. "ONE AT THE _____ AND THE OTHER AT THE FEET."

<u>DOWN</u>

1. "THEN THEY SAID TO HER, '_____, WHY ARE YOU WEEPING?' "
2. " 'THEY HAVE TAKEN AWAY MY _____.' "
3. " 'I DO NOT KNOW _____ THEY HAVE LAID HIM.' "
4. "SHE TURNED AROUND AND SAW JESUS STANDING THERE."

165

RABBONI

FROM: JOHN 20:15-17, NLT

ACROSS

1. " 'DEAR WOMAN, WHY ARE YOU _____?' JESUS ASKED HER."
2. " 'WHO ARE YOU _____ FOR?' "
3. "SHE THOUGHT HE WAS THE _____."
4. " 'IF YOU HAVE TAKEN HIM AWAY, TELL ME WHERE YOU HAVE PUT _____.' "

DOWN

1. " '_____!' JESUS SAID."
2. "SHE TURNED TO HIM AND CRIED OUT, 'RABBONI!' "
3. " 'GO FIND MY _____.' "
4. " 'TELL THEM, "I AM ASCENDING TO MY FATHER AND YOUR FATHER, TO MY _____ AND YOUR GOD." ' "

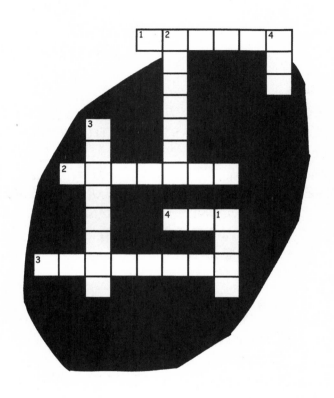

167

DOUBTING THOMAS

FROM: JOHN 20:24–29, NLT

ACROSS

1. "ONE OF THE TWELVE DISCIPLES, _____ (NICK-NAMED THE TWIN), WAS NOT WITH THE OTHERS WHEN JESUS CAME."
2. "THEY TOLD HIM, 'WE HAVE SEEN THE _____!' "
3. "HE REPLIED, 'I WON'T BELIEVE IT UNLESS I SEE THE _____ WOUNDS IN HIS HANDS.' "
4. "JESUS WAS STANDING AMONG THEM. '_____ BE WITH YOU,' HE SAID."

DOWN

1. "HE SAID TO THOMAS, 'PUT YOUR _____ HERE.' "
2. A NICKNAME OF THE DISCIPLE THOMAS'S IS _____ THOMAS.
3. "JESUS TOLD HIM, 'YOU BELIEVE BECAUSE YOU HAVE _____ ME.' "
4. " '_____ ARE THOSE WHO BELIEVE WITHOUT SEEING ME.' "

169

BELIEVE IN THE ONE

JOHN 20:30–31, KJV

USING THE UNDERLINED WORDS BELOW,
FILL IN THE BOXES ON THE NEXT PAGE.

"AND MANY <u>OTHER</u> SIGNS TRULY DID JESUS
IN THE <u>PRESENCE</u> OF HIS DISCIPLES, WHICH
ARE NOT <u>WRITTEN</u> IN THIS BOOK."

"BUT THESE ARE WRITTEN, THAT YE <u>MIGHT</u>
<u>BELIEVE</u> THAT JESUS IS THE <u>CHRIST</u>, THE
<u>SON</u> OF GOD; AND THAT BELIEVING YE
MIGHT HAVE <u>LIFE</u> THROUGH HIS <u>NAME</u>."

WHAT IS PRAYER?

SO MANY OF US MAKE PRAYER MORE DIFFICULT THAN IT NEEDS TO BE.

WE'RE ALWAYS WONDERING *WHEN* AND *HOW* WE SHOULD PRAY. SHOULD I PRAY ON MY KNEES OR WHILE I'M SITTING OR STANDING? SHOULD I PRAY IN PUBLIC OR SHOULD I PRAY IN PRIVATE? DO I PRAY FOR MY NEEDS OR THE NEEDS OF OTHERS? DO I PRAY CONSISTENTLY ABOUT SOMETHING OR DO I ASK ONLY ONCE AND TRUST THAT GOD WILL ANSWER?

WHAT SHOULD MY *ATTITUDE* BE WHEN I PRAY? WHAT DOES IT MEAN, TO "PRAY IN THE SPIRIT"? DO I PRAY ACCORDING TO GOD'S WILL? *HOW DO I KNOW GOD'S WILL?*

TOO MANY OF US THINK THAT PRAYER IS A WAY TO GET WHAT WE WANT OR IS SOMETHING WE DO TO BE MORE SPIRITUAL. DO WE SEE GOD AS A "GREAT VENDING MACHINE IN THE SKY" OR DO WE REDUCE PRAYER TO A FORMULA TO FOLLOW SO THAT WE MAY APPROACH GOD?

TO ANSWER ALL THESE QUESTIONS, LET'S LOOK TO GOD AND HIS WORD. AS YOU GO THROUGH THIS BOOK, SIMPLY ASK GOD TO SHOW YOU *HIS* TRUTH ABOUT PRAYER!

BE FAITHFUL IN PRAYER

ROMANS 12:9-13

ACROSS

1. "LOVE   MUST   BE   _____."
2. "HATE WHAT IS EVIL; _____ TO WHAT IS GOOD."
3. "BE DEVOTED TO ONE _____ IN BROTHERLY LOVE."
4. "HONOR   ONE   ANOTHER   _____ YOURSELVES."

DOWN

1. "NEVER BE _____ IN ZEAL."
2. "BUT KEEP YOUR _____ FERVOR."
3. "_____ THE LORD."
4. "BE   JOYFUL   IN   HOPE,   PATIENT   IN AFFLICTION, FAITHFUL IN _____."

DEVOTE YOURSELVES TO PRAYER

ACTS 2:42

USING THE UNDERLINED WORDS BELOW,
FILL IN THE BOXES ON THE NEXT PAGE.

"THEY <u>DEVOTED</u> <u>THEMSELVES</u> TO THE <u>APOSTLES</u>' <u>TEACHING</u> AND TO <u>THE</u> <u>FELLOWSHIP</u>, TO THE <u>BREAKING</u> OF <u>BREAD</u> AND TO PRAYER."

WHAT DID JESUS DO?

USING THE WORDS LISTED BELOW, FILL
IN THE BOXES ON THE NEXT PAGE.

HEALED
SPREAD
PLACES
PRAYED
HEAR
CROWDS

JESUS
WITHDREW
PEOPLE
NEWS
SICKNESSES
LONELY

HE PRAYED

FROM: MARK 1:34–35, NKJV

ACROSS

1. "THEN HE HEALED MANY WHO WERE SICK WITH
   _____ DISEASES."
2. "AND CAST OUT _____ DEMONS."
3. "AND _____ DID NOT ALLOW THE DEMONS TO
   SPEAK."
4. "_____ THEY KNEW HIM."

DOWN

1. NOT LATE.
2. "HAVING RISEN A LONG _____ BEFORE
   DAYLIGHT."
3. A BUILDING THAT A FAMILY LIVES IN.
4. "HE WENT OUT AND DEPARTED TO A SOLITARY
   _____."

SEEKING GOD'S DIRECTION

FROM: LUKE 6:12–15, NIRV

ACROSS

1. "ON ONE OF THOSE DAYS, JESUS WENT OUT TO A _____ TO PRAY."
2. "HE _____ THE NIGHT PRAYING TO GOD."
3. "WHEN _____ CAME, HE CALLED FOR HIS DISCIPLES TO COME TO HIM."
4. HOW MANY DISCIPLES DID JESUS CHOOSE?

DOWN

1. "AND MADE THEM _____."
2. "_____ WAS ONE OF THEM. JESUS GAVE HIM THE NAME PETER."
3. "_____, SON OF ALPHAEUS."
4. "SIMON WHO WAS CALLED THE _____."

183

HE WAS ALONE

MATTHEW 14:22-23

ACROSS

1. "IMMEDIATELY JESUS MADE THE _____."
2. "GET _____ THE BOAT."
3. "AND GO ON _____ OF HIM TO THE OTHER SIDE."
4. "WHILE HE _____ THE CROWD."

DOWN

1. "AFTER HE HAD _____THEM."
2. "HE WENT UP ON A _____ BY HIMSELF TO PRAY."
3. "WHEN _____ CAME."
4. "HE WAS _____ ALONE."

THE FATHER ALWAYS HEARS ME

JOHN 11:42-43

USING THE UNDERLINED WORDS BELOW, FILL IN THE BOXES ON THE NEXT PAGE.

"'I <u>KNEW</u> THAT YOU <u>ALWAYS</u> HEAR ME, BUT I SAID THIS FOR THE <u>BENEFIT</u> OF THE <u>PEOPLE</u> <u>STANDING</u> HERE, THAT THEY MAY <u>BELIEVE</u> THAT YOU <u>SENT</u> ME.'"

"<u>WHEN</u> HE HAD SAID THIS, <u>JESUS</u> <u>CALLED</u> IN A LOUD VOICE, '<u>LAZARUS</u>, COME OUT!'"

HE GIVES ME WHAT I ASK FOR

JOHN 11:21–22

USING THE UNDERLINED WORDS BELOW,
FILL IN THE BOXES ON THE NEXT PAGE.

"'<u>LORD</u>,' <u>MARTHA</u> SAID TO <u>JESUS</u>, 'IF YOU
HAD <u>BEEN</u> <u>HERE</u>, MY <u>BROTHER</u> <u>WOULD</u> NOT
HAVE <u>DIED</u>. BUT I <u>KNOW</u> <u>THAT</u> <u>EVEN</u> NOW
<u>GOD</u> WILL GIVE YOU <u>WHATEVER</u> YOU <u>ASK</u>.'"

ASK YOURSELF

WHAT HAVE YOU LEARNED SO FAR? FIND OUT
BY ANSWERING THE QUESTIONS BELOW.

1. WHAT ARE WE TO DEVOTE
OURSELVES TO?

COLOSSIANS 4:2

_____

2. WHAT ATTITUDES SHOULD WE
HAVE WHEN WE PRAY?

COLOSSIANS 4:2

_____

3. WHAT ARE WE TO BE FAITHFUL IN?

ROMANS 12:12

_____

4. HOW LONG DID JESUS SPEND PRAYING TO HIS FATHER?

LUKE 6:12–16

_____

5. WHERE DID JESUS GO AFTER HE DISMISSED THE CROWDS?

MATTHEW 14:23

_____

6. WHY DID JESUS GO TO THE MOUNTAINSIDE?

MATTHEW 14:23

_____

THE LORD'S PRAYER

FROM: JOHN 17:1–5, NASB

ACROSS

1. " '_____, THE HOUR HAS COME.' "
2. " '_____ YOUR SON, THAT THE SON MAY GLORIFY YOU.' "
3. " 'YOU GAVE HIM AUTHORITY _____ ALL FLESH.' "
4. " 'THIS IS _____ LIFE, THAT THEY MAY KNOW YOU.' "

DOWN

1. " 'I GLORIFIED YOU ON THE _____.' "
2. ANOTHER WORD FOR FINISHING.
3. " 'NOW, FATHER, _____ ME TOGETHER WITH YOURSELF.' "
4. " 'WITH THE GLORY WHICH I HAD WITH YOU BEFORE THE _____ WAS.' "

193

I PRAY FOR MY DISCIPLES

FROM: JOHN 17:6–8

ACROSS

1. "'I HAVE _____ YOU TO THOSE WHOM YOU GAVE ME OUT OF THE WORLD.'"
2. "'THEY WERE YOURS; YOU GAVE THEM TO ME AND THEY HAVE _____ YOUR WORD.'"
3. "'NOW THEY KNOW THAT _____.'"
4. "'YOU HAVE _____ ME COMES FROM YOU.'"

DOWN

1. "'FOR I _____ THEM THE WORDS YOU GAVE ME.'"
2. "'AND THEY _____ THEM.'"
3. "'THEY KNEW WITH _____ THAT I CAME FROM YOU.'"
4. "'AND THEY BELIEVED THAT YOU _____ ME.'"

195

PROTECT THEM

FROM: JOHN 17:11–15, NLT

ACROSS

1. TO STAY.
2. " 'NOW I AM DEPARTING FROM THE _____.' "
3. " 'NOW _____ THEM BY THE POWER OF YOUR NAME.' "
4. " 'YOU HAVE GIVEN ME YOUR _____.' "

DOWN

1. WHEN WE TALK TO GOD, WE COME TO HIM IN _____.

2. " 'I'M NOT ASKING YOU TO TAKE THEM OUT OF THE _____.' "
3. NOT THIS ONE, BUT _____ ONE.
4. " 'KEEP THEM SAFE FROM THE EVIL _____.' "

197

THAT THEY MAY HAVE MY JOY

USING THE WORDS LISTED BELOW, FILL IN THE BOXES ON THE NEXT PAGE.

HATED
MORE
THINGS
COMING
FULL
JOY

WORLD
MEASURE
GIVEN
WORLD
STILL
WORD

SANCTIFY THEM

USING THE WORDS LISTED BELOW, FILL IN THE BOXES ON THE NEXT PAGE.

SENT
SANCTIFIED
WORLD
TRULY
MYSELF
NOT

WORLD
EVEN
NOT
SANCTIFY
TRUTH
WORLD

UNITY WITH CHRIST

FROM: JOHN 17:21–23, NKJV

ACROSS

1. " '_____ ALSO MAY BE ONE IN US.' "
2. " 'THE WORLD MAY _____ THAT YOU SENT ME.' "
3. " 'AND THE _____ WHICH YOU GAVE ME I HAVE GIVEN THEM.' "
4. " 'THAT THEY ALL MAY BE _____, AS YOU, FATHER, ARE IN ME, AND I IN YOU.' "

DOWN

1. " 'I IN _____, AND YOU IN ME.' "
2. IF I DID ALREADY BRING SOMETHING, I _____ IT.
3. " 'AND HAVE _____ THEM.' "
4. " 'AS _____ HAVE LOVED ME.' "

TO BE WITH ME

USING THE WORDS LISTED BELOW, FILL
IN THE BOXES ON THE NEXT PAGE.

GLORY
BEFORE
TO
THOSE
WORLD
GIVEN

FATHER
WANT
BECAUSE
LOVED
WITH
CREATION

I WILL BE IN THEM

FROM: JOHN 17:25–26, ESV

ACROSS

1. " 'O _____ FATHER.' "
2. " 'THE WORLD _____ NOT KNOW YOU.' "
3. " 'I _____ YOU.' "
4. " 'THESE KNOW THAT YOU HAVE _____ ME.' "

DOWN

1. " 'I MADE _____ TO THEM YOUR NAME.' "
2. " 'I WILL _____ TO MAKE IT KNOWN.' "
3. ME, _____, AND I.
4. " 'THE LOVE WITH WHICH YOU HAVE LOVED ME
   MAY BE IN _____, AND I IN THEM.' "

207

ASK YOURSELF

WHAT HAVE YOU LEARNED SO FAR? FIND OUT
BY ANSWERING THE QUESTIONS BELOW.

1. WHAT DID JESUS ASK HIS FATHER
   TO DO?

   JOHN 17:1

   _____

2. WHY DID JESUS WANT TO BE
   GLORIFIED?

   JOHN 17:1

   _____

3. WHAT DID JESUS SAY ETERNAL
   LIFE WAS?

   JOHN 17:3

   _____

4. WHO IS JESUS PRAYING FOR?

JOHN 17:20

_____

5. WHAT WAS JESUS' PRAYER FOR THOSE WHO BELIEVED?

JOHN 17:21–23

_____

6. WHAT DID JESUS WANT FOR THOSE THE FATHER HAD GIVEN HIM?

JOHN 17:24

_____

THRONE OF GRACE

HEBREWS 4:16

USING THE UNDERLINED WORDS BELOW,
FILL IN THE BOXES ON THE NEXT PAGE.

"<u>LET</u> US THEN <u>APPROACH</u> THE <u>THRONE</u> OF
<u>GRACE</u> <u>WITH</u> <u>CONFIDENCE</u>, SO THAT WE
MAY <u>RECEIVE</u> MERCY AND <u>FIND</u> <u>GRACE</u> TO
<u>HELP</u> US IN <u>OUR</u> TIME OF <u>NEED</u>."

MOST HOLY PLACE

HEBREWS 10:19-22

ACROSS

1. "THEREFORE, BROTHERS, SINCE WE HAVE
_____."

2. "TO ENTER THE _____ HOLY PLACE BY
THE BLOOD OF JESUS."

3. "BY A NEW AND _____ WAY OPENED
FOR US THROUGH THE CURTAIN."

4. "THAT IS, _____ BODY."

DOWN

1. "AND SINCE WE HAVE A GREAT
_____ OVER THE HOUSE OF GOD."

2. "LET US DRAW NEAR TO GOD WITH A
_____ HEART IN FULL ASSURANCE
OF FAITH."

3. "HAVING OUR HEARTS SPRINKLED TO
_____ US FROM A GUILTY
CONSCIENCE."

4. "AND HAVING OUR _____ WASHED
WITH PURE WATER."

213

BEFORE AND AFTER

USING THE WORDS LISTED BELOW, FILL
IN THE BOXES ON THE NEXT PAGE.

PHYSICAL   ENEMIES
ACCUSATION   ONCE
BEHAVIOR   PRESENT
EVIL   ALIENATED
BLEMISH   RECONCILED

I AM HIS CHILD

JOHN 1:12–13

USING THE UNDERLINED WORDS BELOW, FILL IN THE BOXES ON THE NEXT PAGE.

"YET TO ALL WHO <u>RECEIVED</u> HIM, TO THOSE WHO <u>BELIEVED</u> IN HIS <u>NAME</u>, HE GAVE THE RIGHT TO BECOME <u>CHILDREN</u> OF GOD— CHILDREN BORN NOT OF <u>NATURAL</u> <u>DESCENT</u>, NOR OF <u>HUMAN</u> <u>DECISION</u> OR A <u>HUSBAND'S</u> WILL, BUT <u>BORN</u> OF GOD."

ABBA~DADDY

ROMANS 8:15–16

ACROSS

1. "FOR YOU DID NOT _____ A SPIRIT."
2. "THAT MAKES YOU A _____ AGAIN TO FEAR."
3. "BUT YOU _____."
4. "THE SPIRIT OF _____."

DOWN

1. "AND BY HIM WE CRY, "ABBA, _____."
2. "THE SPIRIT _____."
3. "_____ WITH OUR SPIRIT."
4. "THAT WE ARE GOD'S _____."

219

IN JESUS' NAME

USING THE WORDS LISTED BELOW, FILL
IN THE BOXES ON THE NEXT PAGE.

ENTERED
RECEIVE
FIGURATIVELY
BE
ANYTHING

JOY
WILL
WILL
COMPLETE
UNTIL

ASK YOURSELF

WHAT HAVE YOU LEARNED SO FAR? FIND OUT
BY ANSWERING THE QUESTIONS BELOW.

1. HOW IS GOD'S THRONE
   DESCRIBED?

   HEBREWS 4:16

   _____

2. HOW ARE WE TO APPROACH GOD?

   HEBREWS 4:16

   _____

3. WHEN CAN WE GO TO GOD?

   HEBREWS 4:16

   _____

4. WHAT WILL WE FIND WHEN WE GO TO GOD IN PRAYER?

HEBREWS 4:16

_____

5. DOES A SPIRIT OF FEAR COME FROM GOD?

ROMANS 8:15–16

_____

6. WHAT SPIRIT DO WE RECEIVE FROM GOD?

ROMANS 8:15–16

_____

LORD, TEACH US TO PRAY

LUKE 11:1

USING THE UNDERLINED WORDS BELOW, FILL IN THE BOXES ON THE NEXT PAGE.

"ONE DAY JESUS WAS <u>PRAYING</u> IN A <u>CERTAIN</u> <u>PLACE</u>. WHEN HE <u>FINISHED</u>, ONE OF HIS <u>DISCIPLES</u> SAID TO HIM, '<u>LORD</u>, <u>TEACH</u> US TO PRAY, JUST AS JOHN <u>TAUGHT</u> HIS <u>DISCIPLES</u>.'"

WHAT PRAYER IS NOT

FROM: MATTHEW 6:5–6, NCV

<u>ACROSS</u>

1. " 'WHEN YOU PRAY, DON'T BE LIKE THE _____.' "
2. " 'THEY LOVE TO STAND IN THE _____ AND ON THE STREET CORNERS.' "
3. " 'I TELL YOU THE _____.' "
4. NOT GIVEN, BUT _____.

<u>DOWN</u>

1. " 'WHEN YOU _____, YOU SHOULD GO INTO YOUR ROOM AND CLOSE THE DOOR.' "
2. SOMETHING THAT IS INVISIBLE IS _____.
3. " 'YOUR FATHER CAN SEE WHAT IS DONE IN _____.' "
4. " 'AND HE WILL _____ YOU.' "

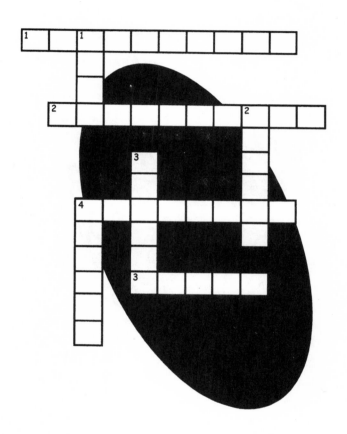

DO NOT KEEP ON BABBLING

USING THE WORDS LISTED BELOW, FILL IN THE BOXES ON THE NEXT PAGE.

HEARD
BABBLING
PRAY
BECAUSE
LIKE

ASK
THINK
BEFORE
PAGANS
FATHER

GOD HEARS MY PRAYER

FROM: JAMES 4:3, 7–8, NASB

ACROSS

1. "_____ ASK AND DO NOT RECEIVE."
2. "_____ YOU ASK WITH WRONG MOTIVES."
3. "YOU MAY _____ IT."
4. "ON YOUR _____."

DOWN

1. NOT OURSELVES, BUT _____.
2. "_____ THE DEVIL."
3. "HE WILL _____ FROM YOU."
4. "DRAW _____ TO GOD AND HE WILL DRAW NEAR TO YOU."

231

MY WORDS ARE IN YOU

JOHN 15:6–8

ACROSS

1. "'IF ANYONE DOES NOT _____ IN ME.'"
2. "'HE IS LIKE A BRANCH THAT IS _____ AWAY AND WITHERS.'"
3. "'SUCH _____ ARE PICKED UP.'"
4. "'THROWN INTO THE FIRE AND _____.'"

DOWN

1. "'IF YOU _____ IN ME AND MY WORDS REMAIN IN YOU.'"
2. "'ASK _____ YOU WISH, AND IT WILL BE GIVEN YOU.'"
3. "'THIS IS TO MY _____ GLORY.'"
4. "'THAT YOU BEAR MUCH FRUIT, _____ YOURSELVES TO BE MY DISCIPLES.'"

233

EVERY WORD OF GOD

USING THE WORDS LISTED BELOW, FILL IN THE BOXES ON THE NEXT PAGE.

WORD   ANSWERED
MAN   GOD
MOUTH   JESUS
EVERY   WRITTEN
COMES   DOES
ON   BREAD

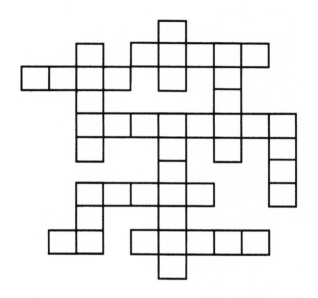

GOD'S WORD IS ENDURING

FROM: 1 PETER 1:22–23, ESV

<u>ACROSS</u>

1. YOU CAN DO IT ALL BY _____.
2. "A _____ BROTHERLY LOVE."
3. "_____ ONE ANOTHER EARNESTLY."
4. "FROM THE _____."

<u>DOWN</u>

1. "SINCE YOU HAVE BEEN _____ AGAIN."
2. "NOT OF _____ SEED."
3. "BUT OF _____."
4. ANOTHER WORD FOR ABIDING OR LASTING.

GOD'S WORD STANDS FOREVER

FROM: 1 PETER 1:24–25, NCV

ACROSS

1. " 'ALL PEOPLE ARE LIKE THE _____.' "
2. " 'AND ALL THEIR GLORY IS LIKE THE _____ OF THE FIELD.' "
3. ANOTHER WORD FOR DIES, AS IN PLANTS OR SHRUBBERY.
4. " 'THE _____ FALL.' "

DOWN

1. " 'BUT THE WORD OF THE _____.' "
2. NOT SITS, BUT _____.
3. "AND THIS IS THE _____."
4. "_____ WAS PREACHED TO YOU."

239

THE WORD OF CHRIST

ROMANS 10:17

USING THE UNDERLINED WORDS BELOW,
FILL IN THE BOXES ON THE NEXT PAGE.

"<u>CONSEQUENTLY</u>, <u>FAITH</u> <u>COMES</u> FROM
<u>HEARING</u> THE <u>MESSAGE</u>, <u>AND</u> <u>THE</u> MESSAGE
IS <u>HEARD</u> <u>THROUGH</u> THE WORD <u>OF</u> <u>CHRIST</u>."

DOUBLE-EDGED SWORD

USING THE WORDS LISTED BELOW, FILL
IN THE BOXES ON THE NEXT PAGE.

THOUGHTS ACTIVE
HEART EDGED
ATTITUDES PENETRATES
SHARPER MARROW
SOUL JOINTS
DIVIDING SWORD

242

GOD-BREATHED

FROM: 2 TIMOTHY 3:14–17, AMP

<u>ACROSS</u>

1. "CONTINUE TO HOLD TO THE THINGS THAT YOU HAVE LEARNED AND OF WHICH YOU ARE _____."
2. "KNOWING FROM WHOM YOU _____ [THEM]."
3. "FROM YOUR CHILDHOOD YOU _____ HAD A KNOWLEDGE OF. . .THE SACRED WRITINGS."
4. SOMEONE WHO USES THEIR KNOWLEDGE IN THE RIGHT WAY IS VERY _____.

<u>DOWN</u>

1. "EVERY _____ IS GOD-BREATHED (GIVEN BY HIS INSPIRATION)."
2. "FOR TRAINING IN _____."
3. "WELL FITTED AND THOROUGHLY _____."
4. "FOR _____ GOOD WORK."

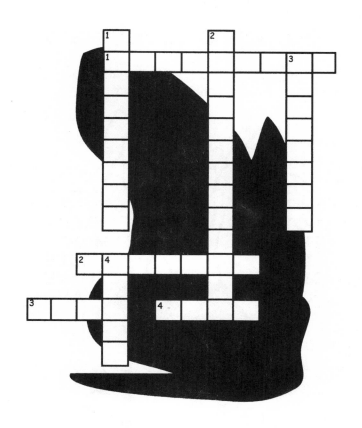

THE WORD GIVES HELP

USING THE WORDS LISTED BELOW, FILL IN THE BOXES ON THE NEXT PAGE.

SPOKEN
NOTHING
THEY
LIFE
GIVES
FOR

COUNTS
FLESH
SPIRIT
LIFE
HAVE
AND

ASK YOURSELF

WHAT HAVE YOU LEARNED SO FAR? FIND OUT
BY ANSWERING THE QUESTIONS BELOW.

1. HOW DID THE HYPOCRITES PRAY?

    MATTHEW 6:5

    _____

2. HOW DID JESUS TELL US TO PRAY?

    MATTHEW 6:6

    _____

3. WHAT WILL THE FATHER DO FOR
   THOSE WHO PRAY IN SECRET?

    MATTHEW 6:6

    _____

4. HOW DID THE PAGANS PRAY?

MATTHEW 6:7

_____

5. WHAT DO PAGANS THINK IT WILL TAKE FOR GOD TO HEAR THEM?

MATTHEW 6:7

_____

6. WHY ARE WE NOT TO BE LIKE THE PAGANS?

MATTHEW 6:8

_____

WHY PRAY?

FROM: PROVERBS 3:5–8, NKJV

ACROSS

1. "TRUST IN THE LORD WITH ALL YOUR _____."
2. "AND _____ NOT ON YOUR OWN UNDERSTANDING."
3. "IN ALL YOUR WAYS _____ HIM."
4. NOT CROOKED.

DOWN

1. "DO NOT BE WISE IN YOUR OWN _____."
2. "_____ THE LORD AND DEPART FROM EVIL."
3. "IT WILL BE _____ TO YOUR FLESH."
4. EATING WELL GIVES OUR BODIES _____.

GOD'S WILL

FROM: PROVERBS 3:5–8, NASB

ACROSS

1. "THESE THINGS I HAVE WRITTEN TO YOU WHO BELIEVE IN THE _____ OF THE SON OF GOD."
2. "SO THAT YOU MAY KNOW THAT YOU HAVE _____ LIFE."
3. "THIS IS THE _____ WHICH WE HAVE BEFORE HIM."
4. THERE IS ONLY ONE TRUE _____.

DOWN

1. "IF WE ASK _____."
2. "_____ TO HIS WILL."
3. "AND IF WE _____ THAT HE HEARS US."
4. "IN _____ WE ASK."

DON'T DO WHAT
PAGANS DO

1 PETER 4:2-3

ACROSS

1. "AS A _____, HE DOES NOT LIVE."
2. "THE REST OF HIS _____ LIFE."
3. "FOR EVIL HUMAN _____."
4. "BUT RATHER FOR THE WILL OF _____."

DOWN

1. "FOR YOU HAVE _____ ENOUGH TIME IN THE PAST."
2. "DOING WHAT PAGANS _____ TO DO."
3. "LIVING IN _____, LUST, DRUNKENNESS."
4. "ORGIES, CAROUSING AND DETESTABLE _____."

THINGS ABOVE

COLOSSIANS 3:1-2

USING THE UNDERLINED WORDS BELOW,
FILL IN THE BOXES ON THE NEXT PAGE.

"SINCE, THEN, YOU HAVE BEEN <u>RAISED</u>
WITH <u>CHRIST</u>, SET YOUR <u>HEARTS</u> ON
<u>THINGS ABOVE</u>, WHERE <u>CHRIST</u> IS <u>SEATED</u>
AT THE <u>RIGHT</u> HAND OF GOD. <u>SET</u> YOUR
<u>MINDS</u> ON THINGS <u>ABOVE</u>, NOT ON
<u>EARTHLY</u> THINGS."

PERFECT AND PLEASING

FROM: ROMANS 1:1–2, NASB

ACROSS

1. A BIBLICAL WORD FOR SLAVE.
2. "PAUL. . .CALLED AS AN _____."
3. "SET _____."
4. "FOR THE _____ OF GOD."

DOWN

1. "HE _____."
2. "WHICH _____ THROUGH."
3. "HIS PROPHETS IN _____."
4. "HOLY _____."

259

HIS PURPOSE

USING THE WORDS LISTED BELOW, FILL
IN THE BOXES ON THE NEXT PAGE.

BLAMELESS
EVERYTHING
TO
ACT
PURPOSE
GOOD

GOD
HIS
SALVATION
OBEYED
ARGUING
ACCORDING

GOOD WORKS

USING THE UNDERLINED WORDS BELOW, FILL IN THE BOXES ON THE NEXT PAGE.

"FOR IT IS BY <u>GRACE</u> YOU HAVE BEEN SAVED, <u>THROUGH</u> <u>FAITH</u>—AND THIS NOT <u>FROM</u> YOURSELVES, IT IS THE <u>GIFT</u> OF GOD—NOT BY WORKS, SO THAT NO ONE CAN <u>BOAST</u>. FOR WE ARE GOD'S <u>WORKMANSHIP</u>, <u>CREATED</u> IN <u>CHRIST</u> JESUS TO DO GOOD WORKS, WHICH GOD <u>PREPARED</u> IN <u>ADVANCE</u> <u>FOR</u> US TO DO."

HELP IN MY WEAKNESS

FROM: ROMANS 8:26–27, ESV

<u>ACROSS</u>

1. "LIKEWISE THE SPIRIT HELPS US IN OUR
   _____."
2. "WE DO NOT KNOW WHAT TO PRAY FOR AS WE
   _____."
3. "THE _____ HIMSELF INTERCEDES FOR US
   WITH GROANINGS TOO DEEP FOR WORDS."
4. NOT ABLE TO.

<u>DOWN</u>

1. "AND HE WHO _____ HEARTS KNOWS THE
   MIND OF THE SPIRIT."
2. "THE _____ INTERCEDES."
3. "FOR THE _____."
4. NOT OUT.

265

ASK YOURSELF

WHAT HAVE YOU LEARNED SO FAR? FIND OUT BY ANSWERING THE QUESTIONS BELOW.

1. WHAT IS THE CONFIDENCE WE HAVE IN APPROACHING GOD?

1 JOHN 5:14,15

_____

2. ON WHAT ARE WE TO SET OUR HEARTS?

COLOSSIANS 3:1

_____

3. ON WHAT ARE WE TO SET OUR MINDS?

COLOSSIANS 3:2

_____

4. IN VIEW OF GOD'S MERCY, WHAT DOES PAUL URGE US TO DO?

ROMANS 12:1

_____

5. WHAT IS IT CALLED WHEN WE OFFER OUR BODIES AS LIVING SACRIFICES?

ROMANS 12:1

_____

6. BY THE RENEWING OF OUR MINDS, WHAT WILL WE BE ABLE TO DISCERN, TEST, AND APPROVE?

ROMANS 12:2

_____

GIVING THANKS

1 THESSALONIANS 5:16–22

ACROSS

1. "BE _____ ALWAYS."
2. "PRAY _____."
3. "GIVE _____ IN ALL CIRCUMSTANCES."
4. "FOR THIS IS GOD'S WILL FOR YOU IN _____ JESUS."

DOWN

1. "DO NOT PUT _____ THE SPIRIT'S FIRE."
2. "DO NOT TREAT PROPHECIES WITH _____."
3. "TEST _____. HOLD ON TO THE GOOD."
4. "_____ EVERY KIND OF EVIL."

HUMBLE DEEDS

JAMES 3:13–16

USING THE UNDERLINED WORDS BELOW, FILL IN THE BOXES ON THE NEXT PAGE.

"WHO IS WISE AND <u>UNDERSTANDING</u> AMONG YOU? LET HIM SHOW IT BY HIS GOOD LIFE, BY DEEDS DONE IN THE <u>HUMILITY</u> THAT COMES FROM WISDOM. BUT IF YOU HARBOR <u>BITTER</u> ENVY AND <u>SELFISH</u> AMBITION IN YOUR HEARTS, DO NOT <u>BOAST</u> ABOUT IT OR DENY THE TRUTH. SUCH 'WISDOM' DOES NOT COME <u>DOWN</u> FROM HEAVEN BUT IS EARTHLY, <u>UNSPIRITUAL</u>, OF THE DEVIL. FOR WHERE YOU HAVE ENVY AND SELFISH AMBITION, THERE YOU FIND <u>DISORDER</u> AND EVERY <u>EVIL</u> <u>PRACTICE</u>."

271

BE DEPENDENT

ROMANS 12:1

USING THE UNDERLINED WORDS BELOW, FILL IN THE BOXES ON THE NEXT PAGE.

"<u>THEREFORE</u>, I URGE YOU, <u>BROTHERS</u>, IN <u>VIEW</u> OF GOD'S <u>MERCY</u>, TO <u>OFFER</u> YOUR BODIES AS LIVING <u>SACRIFICES</u>, <u>HOLY</u> AND <u>PLEASING</u> TO GOD—THIS IS YOUR <u>SPIRITUAL</u> <u>ACT</u> <u>OF</u> <u>WORSHIP</u>."

BE CONFIDENT

USING THE WORDS LISTED BELOW, FILL
IN THE BOXES ON THE NEXT PAGE.

OFFERED
BETTER
HOPE
WELL
RIGHTEOUS

BEING
CERTAIN
COMMENDED
FAITH
STILL

PRAISE HIM

HEBREWS 13:15–16

ACROSS

1. "THROUGH JESUS, _____."
2. "LET US CONTINUALLY OFFER TO GOD A _____ OF PRAISE."
3. "THE FRUIT OF _____."
4. "THAT _____ HIS NAME."

DOWN

1. "AND DO _____ FORGET."
2. "TO DO GOOD AND TO _____ WITH OTHERS."
3. "FOR WITH SUCH _____."
4. "GOD IS _____."

IN THE SPIRIT

EPHESIANS 6:18

USING THE UNDERLINED WORDS BELOW,
FILL IN THE BOXES ON THE NEXT PAGE.

"AND <u>PRAY</u> IN THE <u>SPIRIT</u> ON ALL <u>OCCASIONS</u> WITH <u>ALL</u> KINDS OF <u>PRAYERS</u> AND <u>REQUESTS</u>. WITH <u>THIS</u> IN MIND, BE <u>ALERT</u> AND <u>ALWAYS</u> <u>KEEP</u> ON <u>PRAYING</u> FOR ALL THE <u>SAINTS</u>."

PRAY FOR OTHERS

ROMANS 1:9–10

ACROSS

1. "GOD, WHOM I SERVE WITH MY WHOLE
   _____."
2. "IN _____ THE GOSPEL
   OF HIS SON."
3. "IS _____ WITNESS HOW CONSTANTLY."
4. "I _____ YOU."

DOWN

1. "IN MY _____ AT ALL TIMES."
2. "AND I _____ THAT NOW AT LAST."
3. "BY GOD'S WILL THE WAY MAY BE
   _____."
4. "FOR ME TO _____ TO YOU."

ASK YOURSELF

WHAT HAVE YOU LEARNED SO FAR? FIND OUT
BY ANSWERING THE QUESTIONS BELOW.

1. IN WHAT CIRCUMSTANCES ARE WE
    TO GIVE THANKS?

    1 THESSALONIANS 5:18

    _____

2. WHAT IS GOD'S WILL?

    1 THESSALONIANS 5:18

    _____

3. WHEN WE GIVE THANKS, WHO IS
    OUR FOCUS TO BE ON?

    1 THESSALONIANS 5:18

    _____

4. WHEN WE ARE THANKING GOD, WHOSE NAME DO WE DO IT IN?

EPHESIANS 5:20

_____

5. WHO DO WE GO THROUGH TO PRAY TO GOD?

HEBREWS 13:15

_____

6. WHERE IS OUR FOCUS WHEN WE ARE PRAISING GOD?

HEBREWS 13:15

_____

ASK FOR WISDOM

JAMES 1:5

USING THE UNDERLINED WORDS BELOW,
FILL IN THE BOXES ON THE NEXT PAGE.

"IF ANY OF YOU <u>LACKS</u> <u>WISDOM</u>, HE <u>SHOULD</u>
ASK GOD, WHO <u>GIVES</u> <u>GENEROUSLY</u> TO ALL
<u>WITHOUT</u> <u>FINDING</u> <u>FAULT</u>, AND IT <u>WILL</u> BE
<u>GIVEN</u> TO HIM."

MIND OF CHRIST

USING THE WORDS LISTED BELOW, FILL
IN THE BOXES ON THE NEXT PAGE.

FOOLISHNESS	MIND
HIMSELF	INSTRUCT
LORD	SPIRITUAL
UNDERSTAND	CHRIST
HAVE	BUT

OBEDIENT TO CHRIST

2 CORINTHIANS 10:3–5

USING THE UNDERLINED WORDS BELOW, FILL IN THE BOXES ON THE NEXT PAGE.

"FOR THOUGH <u>WE</u> LIVE IN THE <u>WORLD</u>, WE DO NOT <u>WAGE</u> WAR AS THE WORLD DOES. THE WEAPONS WE FIGHT <u>WITH</u> ARE NOT THE <u>WEAPONS</u> OF THE WORLD. ON THE CONTRARY, THEY <u>HAVE</u> DIVINE <u>POWER</u> TO DEMOLISH <u>STRONGHOLDS</u>. WE DEMOLISH ARGUMENTS AND EVERY <u>PRETENSION</u> THAT SETS ITSELF UP AGAINST THE KNOWLEDGE OF GOD, AND WE TAKE <u>CAPTIVE</u> EVERY <u>THOUGHT</u> TO MAKE IT <u>OBEDIENT</u> TO CHRIST."

HEAVENLY WISDOM

JAMES 3:14-16

ACROSS

1. "BUT IF YOU _____ BITTER ENVY."
2. "AND _____ AMBITION IN YOUR HEARTS."
3. "DO NOT BOAST ABOUT ____."
4. "OR DENY THE _____."

DOWN

1. "SUCH 'WISDOM' DOES NOT COME DOWN FROM _____."
2. "BUT IS EARTHLY, _____, OF THE DEVIL."
3. "_____ WHERE YOU HAVE ENVY AND SELFISH AMBITION."
4. "THERE YOU FIND DISORDER AND EVERY EVIL _____."

DO NOT BE ANXIOUS

FROM: PHILIPPIANS 4:4–7, AMP

ACROSS

1. "_____ IN THE LORD ALWAYS."
2. "AGAIN I SAY, _____!"
3. TENDERNESS OR SOFTNESS.
4. "THE LORD IS _____ [HE IS COMING SOON]."

DOWN

1. "BUT IN EVERY CIRCUMSTANCE AND IN _____."
2. TO GIVE, AS IN A GIFT.
3. "GOD'S PEACE. . .WHICH _____ ALL UNDERSTANDING."
4. "SHALL GARRISON AND MOUNT GUARD OVER YOUR HEARTS AND MINDS IN CHRIST _____."

293

DO NOT WORRY

USING THE WORDS LISTED BELOW, FILL IN THE BOXES ON THE NEXT PAGE.

THEREFORE
ABOUT
RIGHTEOUSNESS
TROUBLE
HEAVENLY
NOT

SHALL
DAY
AS
WORRY
PAGANS
DO

GOD CARES FOR ME

1 PETER 5:6–7

USING THE UNDERLINED WORDS BELOW,
FILL IN THE BOXES ON THE NEXT PAGE.

"<u>HUMBLE</u> <u>YOURSELVES</u>, <u>THEREFORE</u>, UNDER
GOD'S <u>MIGHTY</u> <u>HAND</u>, <u>THAT</u> HE MAY LIFT
YOU UP IN DUE <u>TIME</u>. <u>CAST</u> ALL YOUR
<u>ANXIETY</u> ON HIM <u>BECAUSE</u> HE <u>CARES</u> FOR
<u>YOU</u>."

ASK, SEEK, KNOCK

MATTHEW 7:7-8

USING THE UNDERLINED WORDS BELOW,
FILL IN THE BOXES ON THE NEXT PAGE.

"'<u>ASK</u> AND IT WILL BE <u>GIVEN</u> TO YOU; <u>SEEK</u>
AND YOU WILL <u>FIND</u>; <u>KNOCK</u> AND THE <u>DOOR</u>
WILL BE OPENED TO YOU. FOR <u>EVERYONE</u>
WHO <u>ASKS</u> <u>RECEIVES</u>; HE WHO <u>SEEKS</u>
<u>FINDS</u>; AND TO HIM WHO <u>KNOCKS</u>, THE
DOOR WILL BE OPENED.'"

GO TO GOD

FROM: MATTHEW 11:28–30, NASB

ACROSS

1. IF A PERSON OR ANIMAL IS WEIGHED DOWN, THEY ARE _____.
2. " 'I WILL GIVE YOU _____.' "
3. " 'TAKE MY YOKE _____ YOU.' "
4. " 'AND _____ FROM ME.' "

DOWN

1. " 'FOR I AM GENTLE AND _____ IN HEART.' "
2. " 'AND YOU WILL FIND REST FOR YOUR _____.' "
3. " 'FOR MY _____ IS EASY.' "
4. " 'AND MY _____ IS LIGHT.' "

301

ASK YOURSELF

WHAT HAVE YOU LEARNED SO FAR? FIND OUT
BY ANSWERING THE QUESTIONS BELOW.

1. WHAT ARE WE NOT TO BE ANXIOUS
   ABOUT?

   PHILIPPIANS 4:6,7

   _____

2. WHAT SHOULD WE BRING TO GOD?

   PHILIPPIANS 4:6,7

   _____

3. WHAT DOES THE PEACE OF GOD
   GUARD IN OUR LIVES?

   PHILIPPIANS 4:6,7

   _____

4. WHAT ARE WE TO DO WHEN WE ARE ANXIOUS?

1 PETER 5:7

_____

5. WHY CAN WE DO THIS?

1 PETER 5:7

_____

6. WHO IS THE TRUE SOURCE OF EVERYTHING WE NEED?

MATTHEW 6:31–34

_____

CALL TO GOD

USING THE WORDS LISTED BELOW, FILL IN THE BOXES ON THE NEXT PAGE.

ABUNDANT   ANSWER
CALL   SECOND
UNSEARCHABLE   HEAL
THINGS   GOD
GREAT   KNOW

THE FATHER

FROM: JAMES 2:16–18, ESV

ACROSS

1. "DO NOT BE _____, MY BELOVED BROTHERS."
2. "EVERY GOOD GIFT AND EVERY _____ GIFT IS FROM ABOVE."
3. "COMING DOWN FROM THE _____ OF LIGHTS."
4. ANOTHER WORD FOR CHANGING.

DOWN

1. IF I SELECTED SOMETHING, I _____ IT.
2. WHEN I READ A BOOK FROM BEGINNING TO END, I HAVE READ _____ IT.
3. "THAT WE SHOULD BE A KIND OF _____."
4. _____, SHE, OR IT?

307

MY ATTITUDE

PHILIPPIANS 2:5–8

ACROSS

1. "YOUR _____ SHOULD BE THE SAME AS THAT OF CHRIST JESUS."
2. "WHO, BEING IN VERY _____ GOD."
3. "DID NOT _____ EQUALITY WITH GOD."
4. "_____ TO BE GRASPED."

DOWN

1. "BUT MADE HIMSELF NOTHING, TAKING THE VERY _____ OF A SERVANT."
2. "BEING MADE IN HUMAN _____."
3. "AND BEING FOUND IN APPEARANCE AS A MAN, HE HUMBLED _____."
4. "AND BECAME _____ TO DEATH—EVEN DEATH ON A CROSS!"

WAIT FOR THE LORD

USING THE WORDS LISTED BELOW, FILL
IN THE BOXES ON THE NEXT PAGE.

WAIT
STRAIGHT
STRONG
TAKE
LORD
DESIRE

LIVING
HEART
LAND
BREATHING
GOODNESS
OVER

311

MORE THAN I CAN IMAGINE

EPHESIANS 3:20–21

USING THE UNDERLINED WORDS BELOW,
FILL IN THE BOXES ON THE NEXT PAGE.

"NOW TO <u>HIM</u> WHO IS <u>ABLE</u> TO DO <u>IMMEASURABLY</u> MORE THAN ALL WE ASK OR <u>IMAGINE</u>, ACCORDING TO HIS <u>POWER</u> THAT IS AT WORK <u>WITHIN</u> US, TO HIM BE <u>GLORY</u> <u>IN</u> THE CHURCH AND IN <u>CHRIST</u> JESUS <u>THROUGHOUT</u> ALL <u>GENERATIONS</u>, FOR EVER AND <u>EVER</u>! AMEN."

HE WILL DO IT

JOHN 14:13–14

"'<u>AND</u> I WILL DO <u>WHATEVER</u> YOU <u>ASK</u> IN MY <u>NAME</u>, SO THAT THE <u>SON</u> MAY <u>BRING</u> <u>GLORY</u> TO THE <u>FATHER</u>. YOU MAY ASK <u>ME</u> FOR <u>ANYTHING</u> IN MY <u>NAME</u>, AND I WILL <u>DO</u> IT.'"

HOPE

FROM: ROMANS 15:1–4, ESV

ACROSS

1. "WE WHO ARE STRONG HAVE AN OBLIGATION TO BEAR WITH THE FAILINGS OF THE WEAK, AND NOT TO PLEASE _____."
2. "LET EACH OF US PLEASE HIS _____ FOR HIS GOOD, TO BUILD HIM UP."
3. "BUT AS IT IS _____."
4. IF SOMETHING IS DROPPED, IT HAS _____.

DOWN

1. ALL THINGS TOGETHER IS _____.
2. "FOR WHATEVER WAS _____ IN FORMER DAYS."
3. "THROUGH THE _____ OF THE SCRIPTURES."
4. "WE _____ HAVE HOPE."

317

ABRAHAM

FROM: GENESIS 12:1–3, NASB

ACROSS

1. "THE LORD SAID TO _____, 'GO FORTH FROM YOUR COUNTRY.' "
2. "AND FROM YOUR RELATIVES AND FROM YOUR _____ HOUSE."
3. "AND WILL MAKE YOU A GREAT NATION."
4. "AND I _____ BLESS YOU."

DOWN

1. "AND MAKE YOUR NAME _____."
2. "AND SO YOU SHALL BE A _____."
3. "THE ONE WHO CURSES YOU I _____ CURSE."
4. "AND IN YOU ALL THE FAMILIES OF THE EARTH _____ BE BLESSED."

MOSES

USING THE WORDS LISTED BELOW, FILL
IN THE BOXES ON THE NEXT PAGE.

TELLING	FAVOR
MOSES	FAVOR
NAME	SEND
CONTINUE	WITH
LEAD	REMEMBER
TEACH	PLEASED

PAUL

EPHESIANS 3:16–18

ACROSS

1. "I PRAY THAT OUT OF HIS _____ RICHES."
2. "HE MAY _____ YOU."
3. "WITH _____ THROUGH HIS SPIRIT IN YOUR INNER BEING."
4. "SO THAT CHRIST MAY DWELL IN YOUR HEARTS _____ FAITH."

DOWN

1. "AND I PRAY THAT YOU, BEING ROOTED AND _____ IN LOVE."
2. "MAY HAVE POWER, _____ WITH ALL THE SAINTS."
3. "TO GRASP HOW WIDE AND LONG AND HIGH AND _____."
4. "IS _____ LOVE OF CHRIST."

ASKING OTHERS TO PRAY

COLOSSIANS 4:3–4

USING THE UNDERLINED WORDS BELOW, FILL IN THE BOXES ON THE NEXT PAGE.

"<u>AND</u> PRAY FOR <u>US</u>, TOO, THAT <u>GOD</u> <u>MAY</u> OPEN A DOOR FOR OUR <u>MESSAGE</u>, SO THAT WE <u>MAY</u> PROCLAIM THE <u>MYSTERY</u> OF <u>CHRIST</u>, FOR WHICH I AM IN <u>CHAINS</u>. PRAY THAT I MAY <u>PROCLAIM</u> IT <u>CLEARLY</u>, AS I <u>SHOULD</u>."

ASK YOURSELF

WHAT HAVE YOU LEARNED SO FAR? FIND OUT BY ANSWERING THE QUESTIONS BELOW.

1. WHEN WE WORRY ABOUT THINGS, WHERE IS OUR FOCUS?

   MATTHEW 6:31–34

   _____

2. WHAT ARE WE TO BE SEEKING AFTER?

   MATTHEW 6:33

   _____

3. CAN WE COUNT ON GOD TO MEET ALL OUR NEEDS?

   JOHN 14:13–14

   _____

4. WHAT DOES JESUS TELL US TO DO?
   MATTHEW 7:7

   _____

5. WILL GOD GIVE US ANYTHING BAD
   WHEN WE ASK HIM FOR THINGS?
   MATTHEW 7:11

   _____

6. IN WHAT SITUATIONS ARE WE TO
   PRAY IN THE SPIRIT?
   EPHESIANS 6:18

   _____

FAITHFUL IN PRAYER

USING THE WORDS LISTED BELOW, FILL
IN THE BOXES ON THE NEXT PAGE.

PATIENT
PRACTICE
AFFLICTION
HOSPITALITY
FAITHFUL

PEOPLE
SHARE
JOYFUL
WITH
PRAYER

GOD CREATED

FROM: 1 TIMOTHY 4:4–6, NIRV

ACROSS

1. "EVERYTHING GOD _____ IS GOOD."
2. A HOLIDAY CELEBRATED IN NOVEMBER.
3. ANOTHER WORD FOR SINCE.
4. "_____ WORD OF GOD AND PRAYER MAKE IT HOLY."

DOWN

1. "POINT THESE THINGS OUT TO THE _____ AND SISTERS."
2. ANOTHER WORD FOR PASTOR OR REVEREND.
3. "YOU WERE BROUGHT UP IN THE _____ OF THE FAITH."
4. "YOU RECEIVED GOOD _____."

331

EYES OF THE LORD

1 PETER 3:12

USING THE UNDERLINED WORDS BELOW, FILL IN THE BOXES ON THE NEXT PAGE.

"'FOR THE <u>EYES</u> OF THE <u>LORD</u> ARE ON THE <u>RIGHTEOUS</u> AND <u>HIS</u> EARS ARE <u>ATTENTIVE</u> TO <u>THEIR</u> <u>PRAYER</u>, <u>BUT</u> THE <u>FACE</u> OF THE LORD IS <u>AGAINST</u> <u>THOSE</u> WHO DO EVIL.'"

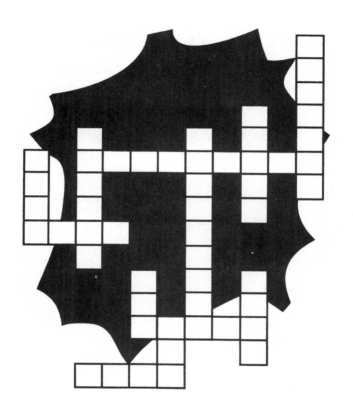

333

ASK YOURSELF

WHAT HAVE YOU LEARNED SO FAR? FIND OUT
BY ANSWERING THE QUESTIONS BELOW.

1. WHAT ARE WE TO PRAY ABOUT?
EPHESIANS 6:18

_____

2. WHO ARE WE TO PRAY FOR?
EPHESIANS 6:18

_____

3. WHEN WE PRAY FOR OTHERS, WHO
ARE WE NOT THINKING OF?
PHILIPPIANS 2:4

_____

4. WHAT DID PAUL URGE TIMOTHY TO DO?

1 TIMOTHY 2:1

_____

5. WHAT LEADERS SHOULD WE PRAY FOR?

1 TIMOTHY 2:2

_____

6. WHY ARE WE TO PRAY FOR OUR LEADERS?

1 TIMOTHY 2:2

_____

PRAYER IS . . .

SO. . . WHAT IS PRAYER? IT IS *TALKING* WITH GOD, WITH OUR HEAVENLY FATHER WHO LOVES US.

PRAYER IS ABOUT GOING TO GOD AND TALKING WITH HIM ABOUT WHAT IS GOING ON IN OUR DAILY LIVES. WE CAN TALK TO HIM ABOUT EVERYTHING AND NEVER DO WE HAVE TO HIDE ANYTHING OR THINK THAT THERE ARE SOME THINGS WE CAN'T BRING TO HIM.

GOD ANSWERS *ALL* OUR PRAYERS. THE ANSWER MAY BE "YES" OR IT MAY BE "NO." AT OTHER TIMES, THE ANSWER COULD BE "WAIT."

PRAYER IS NOT ABOUT US JUST TALKING TO GOD—WE MUST ALSO LEARN TO *LISTEN* AS GOD SPEAKS TO US THROUGH HIS SPIRIT AND HIS WORD.

NO MATTER HOW THE LORD ANSWERS OUR PRAYERS, WE CAN ALWAYS BE SURE THAT HE HAS OUR BEST INTERESTS IN MIND. HE IS OUR LOVING FATHER WHO FAITHFULLY TAKES CARE OF HIS CHILDREN AND HE *ALWAYS* HEARS US AND *ALWAYS* ANSWERS ACCORDING TO HIS WILL AND PURPOSE FOR OUR LIVES.

PRAYER ISN'T SO CONFUSING AFTER ALL, IS IT? IT IS SIMPLY TALKING AND LISTENING TO YOUR BEST FRIEND. . .THE ONE WHO LOVES YOU AND WANTS *ONLY* THE VERY BEST FOR YOU.

FOR YOU. . .HIS CHILD!

ANSWER PAGES

PG. 7

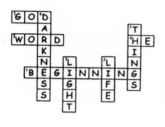

PG. 9

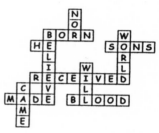

PG. 11

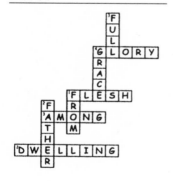

PG. 13

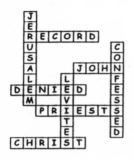

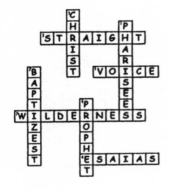

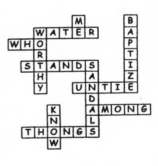

340

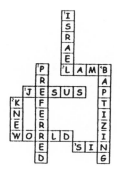

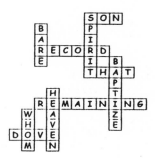

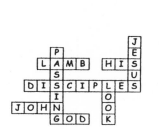

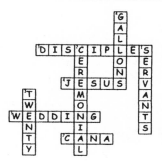

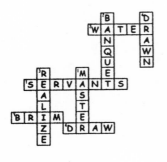

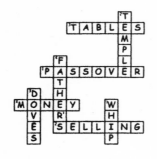

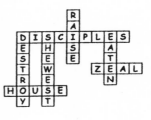

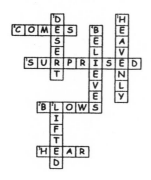

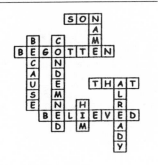

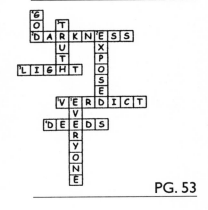

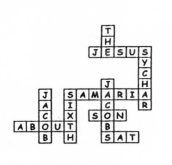

344

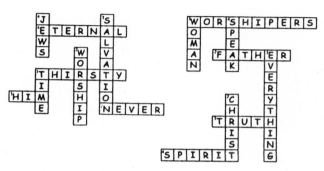

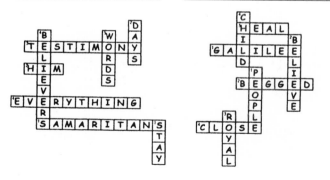

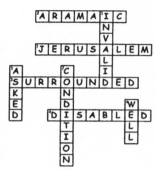

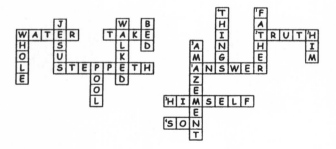

346

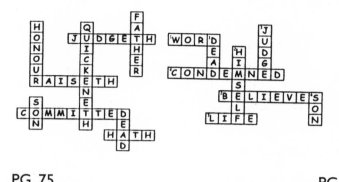

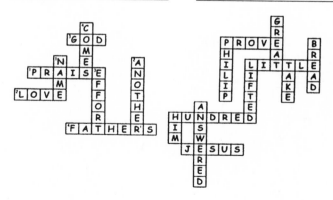

PG. 79

PG. 81

PG. 83

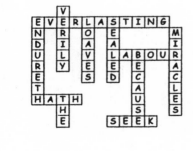

PG. 85

348

PG. 87

PG. 89

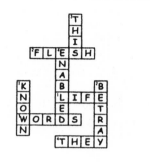

PG. 91

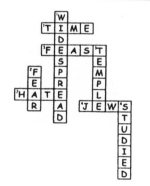

PG. 93

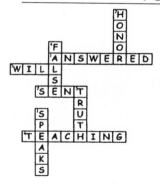

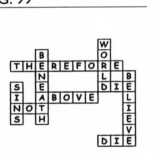 

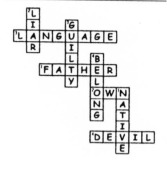

351

PG. 111

PG. 113

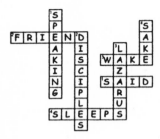

PG. 115

PG. 117

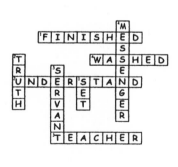

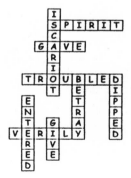

PG. 127

PG. 129

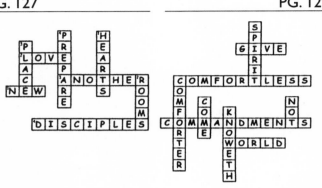

PG. 131

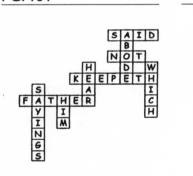

PG. 133

354

PG. 135

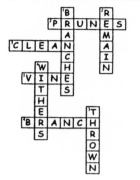

PG. 137

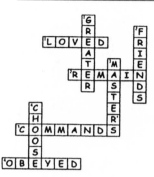

PG. 139

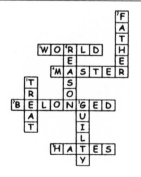

PG. 141

PG. 143

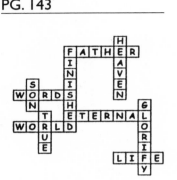

PG. 145

PG. 147

PG. 149

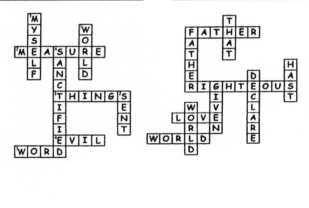

PG. 151

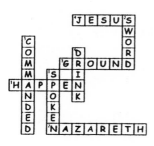

PG. 153

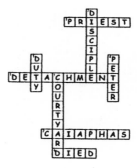

PG. 155

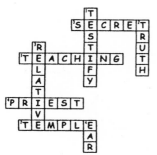

PG. 157

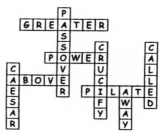

PG. 159

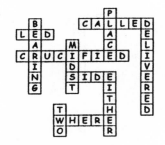

PG. 161

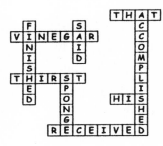

PG. 163

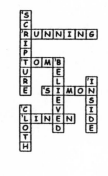

PG. 165

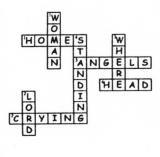

PG. 167

PG. 169

PG. 171

359

ANSWER PAGES

PG. 175

PG. 177

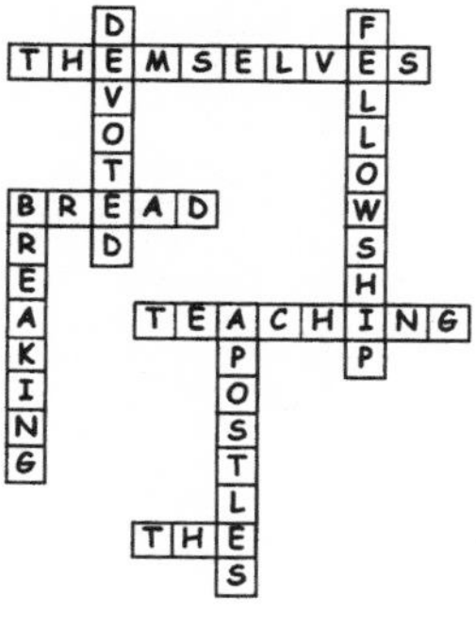

PG. 179

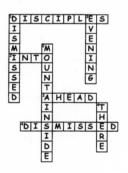

PG. 189

PG. 190–191

ASK YOURSELF
ANSWERS

1. PRAYER.

2. BE WATCHFUL AND THANKFUL.

3. PRAYER.

4. ALL NIGHT.

5. THE MOUNTAINSIDE.

6. TO PRAY.

PG. 193

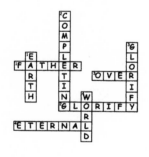

PG. 195

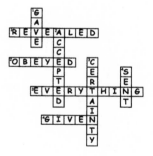

PG. 197

PG. 199

PG. 201

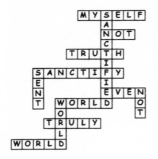

PG. 203

PG. 205

PG. 207

PG. 208–209

ASK YOURSELF
ANSWERS

1. TO GLORIFY HIS SON.

2. TO GLORIFY THE FATHER.

3. TO KNOW THE FATHER AND CHRIST.

4. FOR THOSE WHO BELIEVE.

5. THAT THEY MAY BE ONE.

6. TO BE WITH HIM AND SEE HIS GLORY.

PG. 211

PG. 213

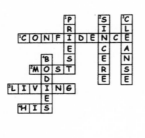

PG. 215

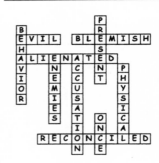

PG. 217

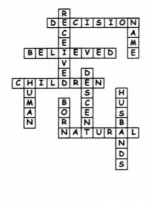

PG. 219

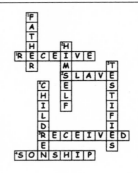

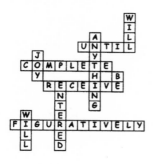

TEST YOURSELF
ANSWERS

1. THE THRONE OF GRACE.

2. WITH CONFIDENCE.

3. IN OUR TIME OF NEED.

4. GRACE TO HELP US.

5. NO.

6. THE SPIRIT OF SONSHIP.

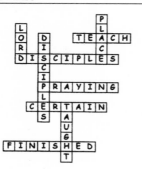

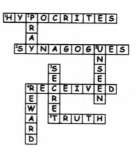

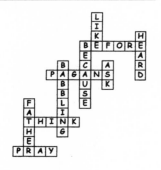

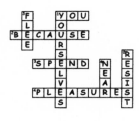

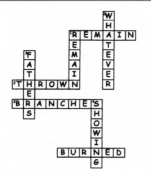

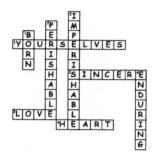

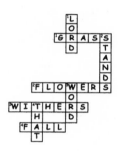

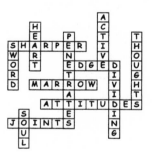

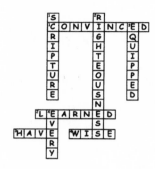

ASK YOURSELF
ANSWERS

1. TO BE SEEN BY MEN.

2. IN SECRET.

3. WILL REWARD THEM.

4. THEY KEPT ON BABBLING.

5. THEIR MANY WORDS.

6. GOD KNOWS WHAT WE NEED BEFORE WE EVEN ASK HIM!

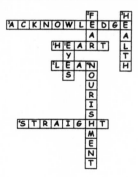

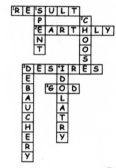

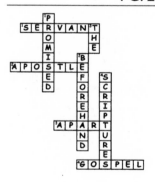

371

PG. 261

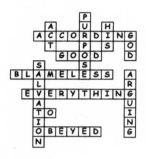

PG. 263

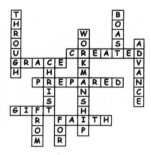

PG. 265

PG. 266–267

ASK YOURSELF
ANSWERS

1. TO ASK ANYTHING ACCORDING TO HIS WILL.

2. ON THINGS ABOVE.

3. ON THINGS ABOVE.

4. OFFER OUR BODIES AS LIVING SACRIFICES.

5. OUR SPIRITUAL ACT OF WORSHIP.

6. WHAT GOD'S WILL IS.

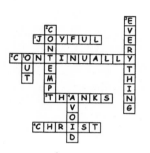

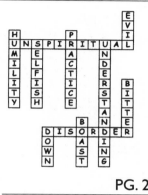

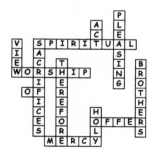

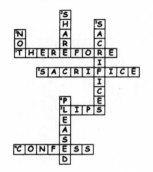

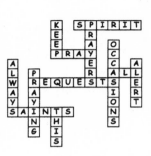

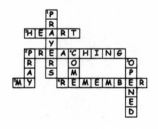

ASK YOURSELF
ANSWERS

1. ALL CIRCUMSTANCES.

2. TO GIVE THANKS.

3. JESUS CHRIST.

4. THE LORD JESUS CHRIST.

5. JESUS CHRIST.

6. ON JESUS CHRIST.

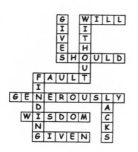

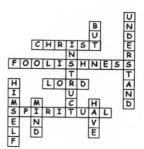

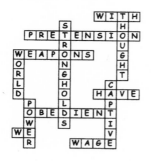

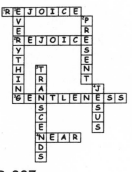

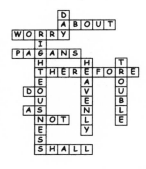

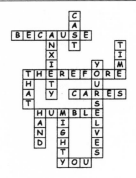

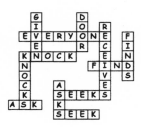

ASK YOURSELF
ANSWERS

1. ANYTHING.

2. OUR REQUESTS.

3. OUR HEARTS AND MINDS.

4. GIVE THE ANXIETY TO GOD.

5. BECAUSE GOD CARES FOR US.

6. THE HEAVENLY FATHER.

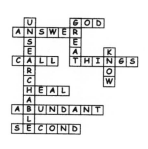

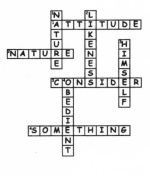

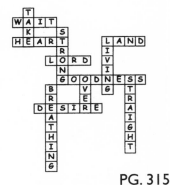

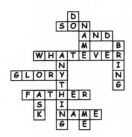

PG. 317

PG. 319

PG. 321

PG. 323

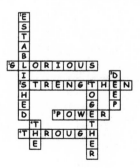

ASK YOURSELF
ANSWERS

1. ON OUR NEEDS.

2. GOD'S KINGDOM AND RIGHTEOUSNESS.

3. YES!

4. ASK, SEEK, KNOCK.

5. NO.

6. IN ALL SITUATIONS.

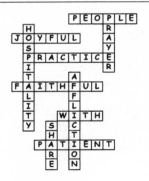

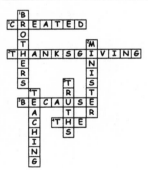

Crossword puzzle:

```
                              A
                              G
                         T    A
                         H    I
         P   R I G H T E O U S
       F R A Y     T    S T
       A A          E
       C Y          N    L
       E R    B     T    O
       E S    U     I    R
              T H E I R  D
         E A R S    V
                    E
```

Words: FACE, EYES, PRAYER, RIGHTEOUS, ATTENTIVE, THOUSE, AGAINST, BUT, THEIR, EARS, LORD

ASK YOURSELF
ANSWERS

1. EVERYTHING.

2. ALL THE SAINTS.

3. OURSELVES.

4. REQUESTS, PRAYERS, INTERCESSION AND THANKSGIVING BE MADE FOR EVERYONE.

5. FOR ALL THOSE IN AUTHORITY.

6. THAT WE MAY LIVE PEACEFUL AND QUIET LIVES.

If you enjoyed
Super Bible Crosswords for Kids,
check out these other books
from Barbour Publishing!

Super Bible Word Games for Kids
ISBN 978-1-60260-392-9

Super Bible Activities for Kids 2
ISBN 978-1-60260-473-5

Super Clean Jokes for Kids
ISBN 978-1-60260-391-2

384 pages of fun in each book. . .for only $5.97!

Available wherever Christian books are sold.